Love Has
Its Reasons

Love Has Its Reasons

An Inquiry into New Testament Love

Earl F. Palmer

WORD BOOKS, Publisher
Waco, Texas

LOVE HAS ITS REASONS

Printed in the United States of America

ISBN #0-87680-481-4
Library of Congress catalog card number: 76-19539

All Scripture quotations, unless otherwise noted, are
from the Revised Standard Version of the Bible, copyrighted
1946, 1952, © 1971, 1973 by the Division of Christian
Education of the National Council of the Churches of Christ
in the U.S.A., and are used by permission.

The quotation from C. S. Lewis on page 11 is from *Miracles:
A Preliminary Study* (New York: Macmillan; London:
Geoffrey Bles; 1947), p. 135 (p. 116, paperback).

To
Arba, Sallee, Mari, Lori, Jim, John
Shirley, Anne, Jon, Elizabeth

Contents

Preface

This book is about love. It is not about a word or words, or about definitions. Rather it is about the event and experience called love. It is an inquiry into the meaning of New Testament love. New Testament love began in the Old Testament. In fact, it goes back to the origins of everything, when God decided to love and to make his love known. Abraham, Moses, and David knew of it and hoped for its fulfillment. Their yearnings, experiences and promises were fulfilled in the person Jesus Christ.

However, I am not primarily interested in a biblical study of love. I have sought, instead, to draw together the experiences of this love within the setting of the first century, which means endeavoring to understand how the Greeks and Romans of the first-century Mediterranean world would have understood New Testament love when its liberating newness first broke in upon them.

What makes this study exciting and relevant for us today in the twentieth century is the fact that God's decision to love still stands in our time with the same healing, fulfilling authority it had at history's beginning or at its center—the redeeming events of Christmas, Good Friday, and Easter.

Writing this book has been a challenging experience for me. In a formal sense the gathering process began in studies, seminars and messages that I have shared at the three churches in which I have served during my ministry as a pastor: University Presbyterian Church of Seattle; Union Church of Manila, Philippines; and my present pastorate, First Presbyterian Church of Berkeley.

My good friend Arba Hudgens has taken on the task of helping me edit and organize this enquiry that has now become *Love Has Its Reasons*. To Arba and his wife Sallee I express my sincere appreciation for their editorial help. I hope this book will be a friendly help to those who wonder about love and its reasons, and to all who have wanted to share in love's way.

EARL PALMER
Berkeley, California

. . . one may think of a diver, first reducing himself to nakedness, then glancing in mid-air, then gone with a splash, vanished, rushing down through green and warm water into black and cold water, down through increasing pressure into the death-like region of ooze and slime and old decay; then up again, back to colour and light, his lungs almost bursting, till suddenly he breaks surface again, holding in his hand the dripping, precious thing that he went down to recover. He and it are both coloured now that they have come up into the light: down below, where it lay colourless in the dark, he lost his colour too.

—C. S. Lewis
Miracles

-1-

A Decision-Event
Love

A rock climber, on a solo climb, in the very last stages of his ascent to the summit, suddenly slips backwards over the mountain's perpendicular drop off. Fortunately, as he falls, he grasps an exposed, protruding root so that he is temporarily spared from a fatal plunge.

Consider his position. He is safe for the present, but he knows that he cannot last long in such a predicament. Inevitably his hands will give out. Either that, or the root will dislodge or break off. He must have help! And the help must be both adequate and immediate. All his present alternatives seem equally disastrous.

Philosophically, one could say that the rock climber's predicament is a characterization of the human situation in the perspective of twentieth-century nihilistic existentialism. There is no real exit. Hopelessness permeates everything.

But continue the parable and complicate it with a new development. Suppose help for the climber does appear at the top of the precipice. Suppose someone peers over the edge and begins to extend a rope down the side of the mountain. Or suppose the rescuer reaches down to the climber and takes hold of his wrists saying, "Let go. I'll pull you up to where you can regain your footing." Will the climber let go of the root and trust the potential rescuer? Think again of his situation. He knows the present state of affairs. He knows he cannot last much longer. But he also knows that to let go of the root means risking everything in favor of the person who makes the promise of help. Will he let go of the root? The answer to that question depends on what the climber thinks of the one who says, "Let go."

The choice is certainly not an easy one. What if he looks up and recognizes the rescuer as, say, a former high school teacher—the literature appreciation teacher whose classroom he and his classmates dismantled halfway through Lord Byron. Will he let go of the root and trust the offered help? Probably in this case the climber would rather take his chances with the mountain. He just doesn't trust the good will of the rescuer regardless of the promise of assistance.

Or think of one other possibility. Suppose a Cub Scout pack is on a tree-identification hike, and one of the smallest boys in the pack hears the cries for help and rushes over to the brink of the precipice. Suppose that, being more kind than realistic, he reaches over the edge and says, "Let go, Mister, I'll help you." Will that offer of help convince the climber to let go? Knowing his own weight and knowing that the crisis is too great for the help being offered, he most certainly will reject the assistance. The root is still his best bet.

What, then, is necessary to persuade the climber to turn loose—to rely on some other source of support? He must be convinced of the good will of the rescuer and of his strength. The assistance offered simply has to be good enough to merit his confidence and strong enough to support his weight. To entrust himself to anything less would be foolishness.

There is a sense in which we all are like the climber gripping the root. We are all clutching at something or some collection of things that give meaning and substance to our lives. But sooner or later our grip on those things tends to weaken. Or the things themselves disintegrate. The root cannot bear so much weight for so long a time. We ask too much of both the root and our hands.

This parable really poses two questions. First, the question of the dynamics of trust: what is it that we as individuals need to know and experience in order to trust ourselves to someone or something?

The second is the objective question of the worthiness of the answers to the meaning of life. There are so many options to look at. There are so many apparent solutions to the huge meaning questions that each of us individually confronts. There are solutions that depend upon our own grip on some source of power. There are the mystical/political/moral discoveries that others have made that we now depend on because of the advocacy of these strong people around us. And then there are the interior solutions which we find or are encouraged to find within our own inner consciousness.

In the pilgrimage of every man and woman these three kinds of discovery are vital to the formation of the human being. But of themselves or even in combination they are not adequate for the kind of ultimate trust that the rock climber needs to pull him back over the cliff. They are not adequate or strong enough for that task. The question then remains, what is?

Not long ago here in Berkeley on the university campus, Alexander Schmemmen, a professor from the Russian Orthodox Seminary in New York, lectured on the life and work of Alexander Solzhenitsyn. He sketched for us the great motivating threads of the writer's life. Solzhenitsyn was a product of the Russian Revolution, a man who had grown up knowing little else but Stalinism. The Revolution was his life. He had trusted his life to Stalin, to Marxism, to the Revolution.

But then Solzhenitsyn experienced a series of great disorienting shocks. One might say he found himself slipping over the precipice. The first came from his army experiences in World War II. Another came after the war when he was imprisoned for political reasons by the Soviet government for the purpose of intellectual reconstruction.

Ironically, it was during this period of attitudinal rebuilding that Solzhenitsyn discovered, or perhaps rediscovered, the great Russian epic authors Dostoevski and Tolstoy. That was the beginning of a pilgrimage which culminated in his finding a new source of meaning, something to which he could trust his life. He discovered the Christian faith.

Father Schmemmen went on to tell us what he considered to be the organizing, fundamental underpinnings of Solzhenitsyn's life and writings, the supporting structures which Solzhenitsyn shares with those monumental Russian writers Tolstoy, Dostoevski, and Pasternak. He described them as Solzhenitsyn's "triune intuition."

The first part of this threefold intuition is the belief that the world, the whole created order, was *made by God*. Because of this insight, he said, Solzhenitsyn and the other Russian epic writers never mock the earth or the human body or any living thing. As they sketch their poignant scenes of the Russian landscape, even as they describe the vast Siberian wastelands, they show a respect for the earth because this first intuition recognizes its good origin. Men and women are also precious. In the novels of these authors, characters may be villainous, as is the brutal father Fyodor in *The Brothers Karamazov*, but even such a raw and chaotic man is never taken lightly nor is his life treated with cynicism. God made the world and all that is in it, even people like Fyodor. God made everything: that's the first intuition.

The second intuition is that men and women, precious as they are, and profoundly meaningful to God (and therefore meaningful to themselves), are in a deep, perplexing *crisis*. The fragmentation of the human personality is faced up to by these Russian writers. This is why there's a true sense of tragedy in their novels. So often in Western twentieth-century novels man is viewed cynically from the outset. Consequently, the ingredients of true tragedy are missing. But these Russian authors view man as worthwhile, so that when he suffers and when he breaks, as he will, a real tragedy occurs. They perceive the human situation to be broken and distorted. Men and women who were made by God, men and women with their good origins, are in a full-scale crisis because of their own sins and also because of the sins committed by others alongside them. A chasm has developed between God and the human order.

When Father Schmemmen came to the third intuition, the standing-room-only audience was completely silent. Solzhenitsyn's third intuition, he said, is his conviction that *the world can be redeemed.* Our life is good because God made each of us. But we are in profound crisis because of our sins, our confusions, our fragmentation, and because of all the things people do to us and the things that we do to other people. Yet redemption of the human situation is possible. This third intuition is rooted in the discovery of God's love—in the discovery of the redeeming event.

Now these may sound like simple, elementary observations. But they are not simple at all. They are not present in the thinking of large numbers of people. Nor do they function as daily working premises in the lives of most men and women. They are not, however, new. The writers of the New Testament saw life in these terms.

The good news of the New Testament is that there is hope, there is someone strong, kind and dependable enough to trust for rescue out of our predicament. Jesus Christ has reached down to where we are and has found us. He has placed his strong hands on our arms and has promised us help.

The New Testament affirms both the good will and the strong authority of Jesus Christ. He is neither the angry figure out of our past who now scolds and threatens us, nor is he the well-meaning but helpless friend. Whether or not we turn loose of the things to which we are clinging and trust the weight of our lives to that promise depends upon our assessment of the extent of our own need and upon our understanding of his strong love. The rest of this book focuses in on the meaning of that love.

All of us come to understand love in our own way, at our own time, at our own pace. In its various forms love is bound to come into our lives and touch and shape us from infancy to the grave. Try as we will, we just can't seem to avoid it. We learn something about love in our early childhood; we seek it all the rest of our lives. We desire it. We need it. Our books, songs, films and television scripts recount endless stories about it. The word seems always to be in the corners of our minds. In Tokyo a Japan Air Lines reservation agent, struggling with the letters of my last name, asked me, when he came to the third letter, "Is that an *l* as in *love?*" Love is a worldwide basic human experience. It is a key word in everyone's vocabulary.

Yet there is hardly a word or an experience that is as misunderstood, or as partially understood, as this one. We have said so much and have written so much about love, it would seem by now that we should have clarified, if not exhausted, the subject. But as Père Teilhard de Chardin observed, a good deal of what has been said concerns only the sentimental face of love. When we consider God's love, we are still usually confused. We seem to have an especially difficult time understanding love as a way of living. And surely not enough has been said to help us clearly understand the unique, life-changing kind of love that unfolds in the New Testament.

I would like to begin this exploration of the Christian understanding of love in the compact Book of 1 John, which the Apostle John wrote as an open letter to the early Christian church. In the final part of his letter, John speaks decisively about love.

> *Beloved*, let us *love* one another; for *love* is of God, and he who *loves* is born of God and knows God. He who does not *love* does not know God; for God is *love*. In this the *love* of God was made manifest among us, that God sent his only Son into the world, so that we might live through him. In this is *love*, not that we *loved* God but that he *loved* us and sent his Son to be the expiation for our sins. *Beloved*, if God so *loved* us, we also ought to *love* one another" (1 John 4:7–11).

Over and over again, some thirteen times in these five sentences, John zeros in on the word *love,* just as Paul does in 1 Corinthians 13. Both John and Paul seem deeply concerned that we who read their letters come to grips with what that word means in the context of the Christian faith.

In the space of these few lines, John emphatically presents the love of God as growing out of a *decision* which God himself has made. That sentence probably sounds a little obscure right now, but let me see if I can clarify what that means. The first thing that John says about love is that it is derived from the will of God. Love is initiated

—love has its existence—because of God's decision to love. Or to put it another way, love springs forth from the very character of God himself. We must begin, therefore, by saying that love, fundamentally, is God's decision.

Notice at the outset what John is *not* saying. He is not saying that love is God. C. S. Lewis handles that point well in his astute little book *The Four Loves*: "John's saying that God is love has long been balanced in my mind against the remark of a modern author (M. Denis de Rougemont) that 'love ceases to be a demon only when he ceases to be a god'; which of course can be re-stated in the form 'begins to be a demon the moment he begins to be a god'. This balance seems to me to be an indispensable safeguard. If we ignore it, the truth that God is love may slyly come to mean for us the converse, that love is God." [1]

It's so easy in our culture to do just this. It's so easy to come up with a definition of love, a concept of love, even an experience of love, and make it our possession. By right of definition we coin the word and even proceed sometimes to deify our definition. C. S. Lewis warns us about that as he continues: "I suppose that everyone who has thought about the matter will see what M. de Rougemont meant. Every human love, at its height, has a tendency to claim for itself a divine authority. Its voice tends to sound as if it were the will of God Himself. It tells us not to count the cost, it demands of us a total commitment, it attempts to over-ride all other claims and insinuates that any action which is sincerely done 'for love's sake' is thereby lawful and even meritorious. That erotic love and love of one's country may thus attempt to 'become gods' is generally recognised. But family affection may do the same. So, in a different way, may friendship." [2]

The New Testament does not teach that love is God. John does not create elaborate definitions or beautiful arrangement of words to describe love and then say, "That's God." Instead, he decisively puts it the other way around. God is love. Love is of God. That is to say, whatever love is, it receives its meaning from God himself. Love, John says, emerges from God's decision. Love is God's will. Love is God's character breaking through. This is what New Testament love is. That is a most significant thing to observe about this special kind of love.

If love originates from the decision God made, what is the implication of that fact? What does it mean to us? The same writer, at the opening of his Gospel account, dramatically affirms that there existed in the beginning of everything the Speech of God, the Word, the Logos. God's character existed from the beginning. God's desire to make himself known was with him right from the first.

In yet another part of the New Testament text, the writer draws out a further implication of this thesis in his song to God the Creator. Listen: "Worthy art thou, our Lord and God, to receive glory and honor and power, for thou didst create all things, and by thy will they existed and were created" (Rev. 4:11).

Now let me put these themes together as they converge from diverse parts of John's writings—from his letters, from his Gospel, and from the Book of Revelation. John says that the world itself was created because of God's love, because of God's decision to love. John portrays love in those same terms in the prologue to his Gospel. Think of it! Because of God's love the world was created. Each of us was made! The thousands of hairs on our heads, the color of our eyes, everything concrete about us and the world in which we live was made because of the love of God. That's a major clue to the New Testament understanding of the love experience.

The implications of this must necessarily shape the way we view the physical world, the way we view our bodies, the way we view each other, and the way we view the whole historical order. God has established the worth of every single person and every single thing. By his love! Here is part of the foundation of the Christian doctrine of ecology. Christians, of all people, must value the earth precisely because the earth, and everything else in the cosmic order as well, originates in God's decision to love. Specifically, because of that love, the world came into being and presently exists.

John makes another major observation about love both in his Gospel and in his short letter. The love by which God decided to create is itself an *event*. John confronts us with this radical statement, "And the Word became flesh and dwelt among us, full of grace and truth" (John 1:14). The Speech of God, his will, his love, was with him in the beginning, and he, Almighty God, made a decision to translate that Speech into a form that we are able to understand.

"In this is love, not that we loved God but that he loved us and sent his Son . . ." (1 John 4:10). God made

[25]

the profound decision to step into the world in the form of a specific man, to intervene in the course of human history at a specific time and in a specific place. He sent his Son to be that actual person in the midst of our crisis, to identify fully with us in life and in death, and to give us victory over death. What is God's love all about? According to John, according to Paul, according to the witness of every other New Testament writer, *love is Jesus Christ.*

Get hold of that last statement. Work with it in your mind. Let it sink deeply into your heart, for it is unquestionably the central teaching of the New Testament. God's love is intensely personal. It comes to us in the form of a person. And Jesus Christ is that person. So often we tend to think of the love of God just as we tend to think of faith or hope—in abstract, theoretical terms. We approach love as though it were an energy or a mood, a sentiment or a cosmic vibration. Or we try to define New Testament love academically, philosophically, theoretically. To do this is to misjudge from the outset the fundamental nature of that love. The love of God is the most personal event in all of history. Because of that amazing love, God became a person.

In his *Mere Christianity*, C. S. Lewis gives us a pointed look at that intensely personal event. "The Second Person in God, the Son, became human Himself: was born into the world as an actual man—a real man of a particular height, with hair of a particular colour, speaking a particular language, weighing so many stone. The Eternal Being, who knows everything and who created the whole universe, became not only a man but (before that) a baby, and before that a *foetus* inside a Woman's body." [3]

The Apostle Paul also moves in on the meaning of love in his letter to the Roman Christians at the end of chapter five. He has carefully explained that as our sin cumulates, as our personal crisis builds in intensity and scope, the love of God increases all the more. He begins the sixth chapter by asking in effect, "Shall we sin more to have more love?" What does Paul have up his sleeve with a question like that?

I think Paul prods his first-century audience with that kind of question because he knows what may be going through their minds. The average person of that era viewed love and faith and hope as though they were ethereal, mystic clouds of divine energy. So Paul's startling rhetorical question is really not so rhetorical.

Look, if God's love is a cosmic force, if it's divine energy, if it flows like an electrical current, if it's a mood or a vibration, then of course there's the possibility that the more we sin, the more love we get. If this is what God's love is all about, then all we really need in life is somehow to get a combination to the lock of this great divine faucet or celestial power line. Wouldn't that simplify things? But, in fact, God's love is radically different from that.

All too often, in our century too, the love of God is mistakenly portrayed by this kind of quantitative imagery. But if we view God's love in these terms, we miss the central fact about it. We miss the mark because we bring love under control of the language we use to describe it. If this were the nature of God's love, if that's all there were to it, then the greatest challenge we faced spiritually would be to learn how to turn this love on and off, how to get it to flow at a desirable rate through our lives. But Paul wisely challenges the Roman Christians not to play word games with the love of God. They are not to sin more to get more of God's love. They don't have to do that because the love of God, the cumulative grace of God, is not an energy, not a sentiment, not a theory or a mood. The love of God is an event! The love of God is a person! The love of God is Jesus Christ! We experience God's love because Jesus Christ, the living Lord, made it possible for us to have a vital, personal relationship with God.

Let me illustrate from our own lives. Like love, suffering is also an event. There is nothing theoretical about it. And because this is so, attempts to help a suffering person with theoretical explanations about the meaning of suffering, even when they are made with genuineness and concern, are usually of very little comfort. For example, the maybe-you're-suffering-because-God-wants-to-teach-you-something approach doesn't really minister helpfully because suffering is an event, and that which really addresses itself to an event is another event alongside it.

A cartoon by Koren in the July 1974 *New Yorker* magazine captures something of this point. A crying child in a park looks hopelessly at his ice cream cone lying splashed on the ground. An adult at the child's side, bending down in tenderness ready to listen, says, "Do you want to talk about it?"

Most human crises are events, and usually other events,

rather than words, are needed to resolve them. Words may play a part, but by themselves they are insufficient.

This is exactly what the New Testament tells us. When God decided to break into history with his own character, when he decided to share his love with the world, he decided to do it in personal, not ideological, terms. He came to us as Word in Flesh, Jesus Christ. Jesus Christ is the love of God breaking through and finding us where we really are. If we really want to know what love is, if we really want to get some kind of handle on the love of God, then we must consider Jesus Christ. We must look closely at him in the New Testament. We must watch him in action. Only then will the love of God begin to become clear to us, and only then will it begin to make a difference in our lives.

Notice a further point from John's words: "In this is love, *not that we loved God* . . ." (1 John 4:10). I don't think most of us really love God even though we may make convincing statements to that effect. We're usually so entrapped in our own self-centeredness that we spend a good deal of our time and energy fencing in our personal territory to protect ourselves from other people and from God too. John calls it like he sees it. We don't really love God as we so often say we do. Our language may be saturated with a lot of sentiment about love. We are forever discussing physical attraction between people. We easily attest to our love of mankind in noncostly, general terms. But John says that we really don't love God. Actually, we don't know how to. John is not condemning us so much as he is stating a plain fact. *But God has loved us.*

God has spoken to us through his Son, and he has come alongside us to redeem us. When we were busily preoccupied with our own affairs, pursuing the loves of our lives—when we were least expecting it—God found us with his love. He has placed his hand upon ours.

God found us with his love. That's a theme that runs throughout C. S. Lewis's children's story *The Horse and His Boy*. In that perceptive book, the boy Shasta, tired, afraid, lonely, barely able to keep his footing on a steep mountain trail, becomes aware of some great figure walking alongside him in the darkness, evidently keeping his horse from stumbling over the precipice. Finally Shasta whispers, penetrating the oppressive darkness with a desperate question, "Who are you?" And the answer comes from the great lion Aslan: "One who has waited long for you to speak." [4] It is then that Shasta hears the story of how the Lion who had chased him, who had both frightened him and protected him at night by the tombs, was the same Lion who had saved his life as a tiny baby and had loved him from the very beginning.

"In this is love, not that we loved God but that *he loved us.* . . ."

What a discovery about love! John discovered it. So did Paul! Thousands upon thousands of others have discovered it too down through the past twenty centuries. Love, says the New Testament, grows out of the decision God made. Love was involved in his decision to create the world, to create mankind, and to redeem individual men and women. All along, love has been his decision. And at a particular point in the course of human history he made that love the central pivotal point of all time. Jesus Christ is that decision-event. He is the love of God. And that love came to us when we weren't even looking for it. It is even called by a special name in the New Testament text: *agapē.*

-2-

Old Words
Won't Do

Since childhood all of us have been formulating and refining our definitions of the word *love*. Our personal experiences with all types of love have been accumulating over all the years of our lives. We approach the subject, therefore, carrying the baggage of a countless number of impressions. We come loaded down with our memories of love—our disappointments, hopes, and fears.

People in the first century were no different. When they were confronted initially by the early church's witness to this new way of being loved and of loving, they had their own conceptions and experiences to deal with. Many previously formed images and impressions undoubtedly swirled through their minds. Those who heard Jesus or the disciples or Paul speak about this new kind of love were not standing around with minds like empty slates. They had already shaped their own understanding of what love is.

Just what kinds of things went through the minds of these first-century people when they thought about love? How did they view love? What words did they use when they talked about it? Our study of love in the New Testament makes questions like these absolutely necessary. We must understand the context into which this new kind of love first was introduced. It is especially important that we explore the first-century Greek mind-set in this regard.

Now obviously the New Testament message was not directed exclusively at the Greek world. All first-century Christians weren't Greek. Jews and Romans and a whole assortment of people were responding to this love in the first century, and that's the way it's been ever since. On the other hand, all the New Testament documents were first written in the Greek language. Furthermore, their vocabulary was heavily influenced by the Septuagint, the Greek translation of the Old Testament which had been written over a hundred years earlier. In no way, therefore, could the New Testament writers escape the existing Greek vocabulary and thought patterns. As we examine, then, the vocabulary and thinking of the first century, we should also be able to find some interesting insights into our own century as well. After all, in a sense, we in Western civilization are children of the Greeks, and Greek culture is an integral part of the underpinnings of Western thought.

Greek is a rich and varied language, with several words for *love*. But of these words, only two exerted much influence in Greek literature and thought in the first century. Two small words, each with a different understanding, conception, connotation, carried the most weight in the Greek world's thinking about love. Both of these words in various forms have worked their way into the English language, so it is fairly easy for us to bring them into understandable focus, to examine their meaning, and to see what light they shed on the New Testament message.

One of these two primary Greek words for love is *philia*. *Philia* might be considered the "garden variety" word for love. It is instinctive love, natural love. It is the love we have for our own bodies and all that is an extension of them—our family, our nation, our tribe, our race. *Philia* is the love that we feel instinctively toward the people and things within our immediate circle, however we may define that circle. It is the love of people to whom we are in some way related. It is the love on which we build a good deal of our personal identity and distinctiveness—even, to a degree, our self-esteem. In a sense *philia* helps us to survive.

Look at some of the ways that word has come into the English language. When attached to the Greek word for brother, *adelphos*, it becomes *philadelphia*, love of brother or sister—a logical name for a city founded by people who believed in brotherly love. Or attach *philia* to the Greek word for wisdom, *sophia*, and it becomes *philosophy*, the love that a person instinctively feels toward wisdom. It is not natural to love foolishness. We naturally feel affection toward wisdom over against error.

Or take *philanthropy*, the love that a person instinctively feels for mankind. That word is formed when *philia* is attached to *anthropos*, the Greek word for man. It is a rare person who does not claim that he or she loves mankind. It may be hard to love specific individual people, but it's instinctive to love people in general. Who can think of a movement in recent times that hasn't proclaimed its allegiance to "the people," to "the masses"? That's a position that few can argue with. It's so basically instinctive.

Incidentally, the verb form *phileō* is used in one part of the New Testament in an interesting way. The disciple John, in his Gospel, refers to himself as the "beloved" disciple, using the verb *phileō* in discussing his special relationship with Jesus (John 20:2). The word choice leads us to believe that John was perhaps the youngest member of the group, the lovable one, the one naturally loved. The older disciples like Peter or Thomas seemed to present more problems. Peter was one of the older apostles, and everybody had problems with him. But few seemed to have problems with John. This title does not imply that he was loved in a deeper sense than the other disciples. There just simply seems to be a natural, instinctive attraction to him. That's what *philia* love is all about.

But there's another word for love that is actually more important in the love vocabulary of classical Greek. It is that mysterious word *erōs*. *Erōs*, like *philia*, has also worked its way into the English language, but we in the twentieth century have usually understood it in one narrow connotation. We have derived from it all kinds of words pertaining to sexual attraction and intrigue with the sexual nature of the self. By doing this, we have lost that larger, more mysterious, even religious, understanding of *erōs* which the Greek language intended.

The Greeks understood *erōs* in a special way. *Erōs* is love that is earned, love that is won from us. It is not the instinctive love that we have for our parents or our children, our family or our social or racial structure. It is not the kind of love we have for something like wisdom or mankind. It is love earned from us because of the compelling excellence of the person or thing or reality. It is the love of beauty, the love of power, the love of strength. It's easy to see, therefore, why *erōs* was used by the Greeks to express religious love. When they thought of love in a religious sense, they thought of their encounter with the divine as an overwhelming experience. When some thing or person so captivated them with its excelling worth, when love was demanded from them by the strength or beauty or the power or the sheer merit of something—that was *erōs*.

Some helpful insights about *erōs* appear in Gerhard Kittel's massive *Theological Dictionary of the New Testament*:

> What the Greek seeks in *erōs* is intoxication, and this is to him religion. To be sure, reflection is the finest of the gifts which the heavenly powers have set in the heart of man . . . ; it is the fulfilment of humanity in measure. More glorious, however, is the *erōs* which puts an end to all reflection, which sets all the senses in frenzy, which bursts the measure and form of all humanistic humanity and lifts man above himself. . . .
> But the intoxication sought by the Greek in *erōs* is not necessarily sensual. Already in the Greek mysteries, as so often in mysticism, erotic concepts are spiritualised in many ways as images and symbols for the encounter with the suprasensual.[1]

In its treatment of *erōs*, the *Theological Dictionary* also probes classical Greek literature to see how the dramatists worked with the intricacies of *erōs* and finds Euripides, for example, saying, "It [*erōs*] is a god, and he is powerful even above the gods."[2] Another states, "All the forces of heaven and earth are forces of second rank compared with the one and only supreme power of *erōs*. No choice is left, nor will, nor freedom, to the man who is seized by its tyrannical omnipotence, and he finds supreme bliss in being mastered by it." [3]

The Bible does not categorically reject this form of love, even though biblical writers purposely avoid the use of the specific word *erōs*. There is a beautiful passage that presents a good example of the Old Testament treatment of the reality of *erōs*. The Hebrew language doesn't have a direct parallel to this Greek word, but it expresses this *erōs* kind of love in several places. One of them is Genesis 24 in which we find a romantic incident beautifully pictured:

> Now Isaac had come from Beer-lahai-roi, and was dwelling in the Negeb. And Isaac went out to meditate in the field in the evening; and he lifted up his eyes and looked, and behold, there were camels coming. And Rebekah lifted up her eyes, and when she saw Isaac, she alighted from the camel, and said to the servant, "Who is the man yonder, walking in the field to meet us?" The servant said, "It is my master." So she took her veil and covered herself. And the servant told Isaac all the things that he had done. Then Isaac brought her into the tent, and took Rebekah, and she became his wife; and he loved her. So Isaac was comforted after his mother's death (Gen. 24:62–67).

That's what romance is. Someone had earned the right to take his mother's place. Paul tells us (quoting Gen. 2:24), " 'For this reason a man shall leave his father and mother and be joined to his wife, and the two shall become one' " (Eph. 5:31). That's romantic love! *Erōs* is at work when a person is drawn away from *philia* by the compelling excellence of another person to form a new relationship. Isaac and Rebekah were caught in the magnetic pull of *erōs*. The beauty, the charm, the grace of Rebekah—these qualities drew Isaac away from meditations in the field. How mysterious and irresistible she was, dressed in those Egyptian cottons and silks. She won his love. That's *erōs!*

We can see several other experiences like this in the Old Testament. The Song of Solomon is primarily about *erōs*, about the senses aroused and delighted by sheer beauty. Nowhere is the *erōs* experience ridiculed or demeaned. It is treated with dignity and respect—even joy. In fact, the word for joy (*chara*) in the New Testament probably comes closer than any other word to expressing the mystery involved in *erōs*.

Both philia and eros[4] capture something of the remarkable nature of the human creature. Philia, the instinctive form of the love experience, the love we feel for that which is an extension of ourselves, by its nature and style preserves and cements and nurtures. It stands against all that threatens the intimate personal or social structures to which it is bound. In other words, philia love tends to be cautious and protective. It becomes part of, or perhaps grows out of, mankind's natural survival mechanisms. This root system love nourishes the family and defends the inner circle against any marauder.

Eros, on the other hand, strains at the boundaries. Eros is men and women desiring and yearning for more. Eros permeates the scene where Rebekah sees the young man in the field; it is there when Isaac first notices Rebekah. Eros is this tremendous force of attraction. It is the yearning for things that uplift the human spirit. It is the love of music, the love of art. It is men and women longing for more than simple existence. Eros is the love of all beautiful things—the love of fulfillment.

The Family of Man is a perceptive photographic study of men and women and children. Edward Steichen collected and arranged the pictures, first for a showing at the Museum of Modern Art in New York and then for the book. One thing that particularly impresses me is the order of the scenes. Near the end of the book Steichen has included several pages of photographs on the pain, adversity and loneliness of the human condition. The brief captions reflect the tragedy of the photographs and repeat the theme up to a final poignant quotation, "Nothing is real to us but hunger." [5] Following this are some seven photographs of human hunger and starvation in India, Africa, Europe, and America.

When I reached this point on my first reading, I wondered what Steichen would dare portray on the page following those terrifying photographs. It seemed almost as if the last word had already been said. Is there anything as real to people as suffering? Isn't food the only thing that makes sense after all? What could be put on the next page?

When I turned the page, I was at first surprised. Then I realized, of course, Steichen was right. With a sentence from Genesis 37, "Behold this dreamer cometh," [6] there appeared a photograph of Arturo Toscanini, conductor of the NBC Symphony Orchestra. "Behold this dreamer cometh!" Eros! The human story involves more than sheer survival. It is more than just being sustained by rice or bread. It involves more than philia. Men and women straining at the boundaries—that's what eros is. It's part of the mark of our humanness. God made us this way. We must have beauty and wonder as well as bread. The fact is, we want it. Philia needs. Eros desires.

Consider the nature of man from a biblical perspective. According to the Genesis record, men and women were created on the sixth day, the same day the animals were created. But we human beings are on the very outer edge of the sixth day. We are not too sure we like being in the sixth day; we're always straining to get over into the seventh day, the one day which, unlike the other six, has no ending. Adam and Eve ate of the tree of life, wanting fulfillment—wanting to be eternal like God.

If we conclude that all we human beings really need is bread, we misunderstand ourselves. We are the part of creation that needs more than bread. We need cathedrals. We need music. We need art. That's the way we are made. And this characteristic contributes both to our greatness and to our crisis.

In 1968 my family and I had the privilege of attending the World Council of Churches meeting in Uppsala, Sweden. From there we traveled on to Russia, India, and then back to our home in Manila. We went to India, among other reasons, to see for ourselves what many people call the most beautiful building in the world. From

[43]

New Delhi we took the drive south to Agra. On our arrival there, we pulled up to an old parking lot muddy with the recent beginning of the monsoon season, crowded with buses and cars and people selling all sorts of things, and headed for an ordinary looking, dark doorway, wide enough to admit only two or three people at a time.

Up to this point on our journey we had not had the slightest glimpse of the famous building we had come to see—no prominent hilltop location to be viewed from afar, no spires or domes or turrets to be seen even from the parking lot. Our son Jon, then two and a half years old, hadn't paid much attention to several of the historical sights we had seen on the trip. The tomb of Lenin, for example, didn't impress him at all. His main interests had been a teddy bear and a small collection of favorite toys. But as Jon walked through that narrow doorway with the rest of us, he actually gasped at the sight before his eyes. There it was—like a vivid Kodachrome slide projected in a dark room—the Taj Mahal! For an amazing instant it took his breath away.

That incident helped me to realize more clearly than ever that my son is a human being, not an animal designed only to survive, to eat, to work. He is a person. He loves beauty. He is capable of responding to it. He is capable of experiencing eros. He needs it. He will want it all his life.

But both philia and eros present a problem to us. Each contains an inherent weakness. Neither of them, of themselves or even together, provides an adequate or safe foundation on which to build a truly human existence.

Neither of them will support the total weight of a person's life. That's their dilemma. That's their fatal shortcoming.

Philia love, to be sure, has some marvelous qualities. Developing intimate bonds within the family and establishing relationships in our circle of friends and in our community is rightly honored. Building protective barriers is, to a degree, both physically and psychologically necessary. We recoil at stories of those who walk away from the blood ties of the family and ignore parents or children as if they did not exist. But basically this love, when it stands in isolation, inevitably will turn inward toward the self. That's its primary problem. "For whoever would save his life will lose it," says Jesus (Matt. 16:25). He is here touching on the deadening stagnation that haunts philia love when it becomes the sole motivation in a person's life.

The love of a mother and father for their children is an indescribably beautiful and touching thing. So is a child's love for his or her parents. And who wants to find fault with brotherly love? But in the end even this beautiful, fulfilling, necessary kind of love—this philia love—turns out to be an unstable foundation for supporting our lives. Finally our children leave; finally our parents pass away; finally our closest associations dissolve. Time does it to us.

Philia is like a plant in a flower pot. A California redwood tree may, for instance, be put into a clay pot, and it will grow well for a while. But it is sure to become rootbound. Philia, alone, eventually becomes rootbound. Great as it is, it's not big enough to support all of life, to give substantial meaning to all of living, to integrate all the parts of the whole. We can love our race and be caught up in a black-is-beautiful or yellow-is-beautiful or white-is-beautiful philosophy, but Jesus warns us about anchoring our whole life to that sort of thing. Racial love, like other forms of philia love, eventually stagnates, becomes myopic, and even tends toward self-destruction. Sooner or later it becomes rootbound.

Eros, too, presents its own set of problems. Eros by itself is no safe foundation on which to build. Fascinated as it is with beauty and power, in the long run eros has a dehumanizing effect. You see, eros love is directed only toward that which is smart and charming and beautiful. It's wonderful to love Beethoven's Fifth Symphony or the Taj Mahal or Mount Shasta or Niagara Falls. In fact, there would be something wrong with a person if, upon seeing Niagara Falls for the first time, he were to say something like, "It's cute," or "If you've seen one water-fall, you've seen them all." Insipid remarks like those are totally out of place. Our senses should be dazzled by things that are strong and powerful and charming. But as a fundamental foundation for our lives, eros is inadequate. Why? Because eros by nature avoids too much. It avoids tragedy. It avoids pain and hurt. It avoids plainness and unpleasantness. It avoids long-term commitment and the really important costly relationships of life.

Our own generation has many of the marks of an eros generation. There is a tendency today for us to pay most attention to people who are able to help us on our way up! But the people on their way down we'll usually drop as fast as we can. We all too readily avoid any load that proves too inconvenient or heavy to carry. If other people don't fit into our self-interests, if they are not able to impress us, then we tend to move away from them. That's eros; it is desire-oriented. It quickly produces in-crowds and out-crowds.

Eros even causes us to begin to view every other human being as a potential threat to our own full actualization. Therefore, it has within it no basis for ethics or long-term concern for the ordinary people who daily come into our lives. So few people—so few things—are really beautiful enough to merit, to demand, our full attention. The result is an ever-shrinking circle of those things and people which are able to please us. Therefore, like philia, eros inevitably moves toward the stagnation which Jesus spoke against. "Whoever would save his life will lose it." It eventually ends up in endless preoccupation with the self, with beauty, with that which is currently in vogue, and there is no solid footing in that.

Both eros and philia need a greater setting in which to become meaningful. And there *is* that greater context. There is the special kind of love that the Bible speaks about—the love that is more far-reaching and substantial than either philia or eros. It is a kind of love that is big enough, strong enough, stable enough to encompass both. It is able to make sense out of these two yearnings of our hearts without discrediting or dismissing them. It is that love that became real to people like Paul and John. *Agapē*, they called it.

-3-

The New Word for the New Love

When the New Testament writers (as the Septuagint translators before them) came to write about these new dimensions of love, they found the existing Greek love vocabulary inadequate for their purposes. *Philia* and *erōs* simply lacked the capacity to convey the quality, the scope, the depth of the love they had discovered in God's revelation. As a result, these writers seem to have gone out of their way to suppress these two standard words for *love* (with their related verb forms) in their writings. The verb *phileō* does frequently appear in the New Testament and in the Septuagint, and the noun *philia* is used once (James 4:4). But *erōs* with its religious connotations, its implication of being overpowered by the gods, seemed totally inappropriate for expressing the love relationship between the God of creation and redemption, on the one hand, and mankind, on the other. So these writers searched for a different word to capture the essence, the impact, of this new love. Their search led them to *agapē*.

Agapē is a word used only sparingly in classical Greek. In fact, the noun form has been found in only four separate places in all of the known classical Greek writings. According to Kittel's *Theological Dictionary of the New Testament, agapē* "is often a mere synonym which is set alongside the other two for the sake of emphasis or stylistic variation." [1] Its meaning is vague and colorless. In a general sense, *agapē* comes close to meaning "good will."

The New Testament writers decided to take the same linguistic approach that the Septuagint writers had taken more than a hundred years before. They seized hold of this bland, little-known, imprecise word *agapē* and loaded it with their own meaning. Note Kittel's work again. The Septuagint "almost always renders the *ohab* of the Hebrew text by *agapan* [the verb form]. *Erōs* and *philia* and derivatives are strongly suppressed. The harmless *agapan* carries the day, mainly because by reason of its prior history it is the best adapted to express the thoughts of selection, of willed address and of readiness for action. But the true victor is the ancient *ohab* which impresses upon the colourless Greek word its own rich and strong meaning." [2] *Agapē*, then, derives its definition from the Old Testament view of God's strong and faithful love, and from its function in the New Testament text, not from Greek culture and thought.

Now I don't want to be misleading. The New Testament writers do not reject the kinds of love depicted by *philia* and *erōs*. Not at all. They, instead, seem to place both our human love, our instinctive love for all that is an extension of ourselves, as well as our yearnings for beauty and fulfillment, into a greater context. Observe how this is done in one of the most classic portions of the New Testament, 1 Corinthians 13.

In the opening paragraph of this hymn to love, Paul poses a series of rhetorical statements, all of them centering on the loves and the virtues of our lives. He points out that these loves and virtues of themselves, as great and significant as they are, do not have enough substance to function alone. They need some deeper reality, some greater truth from which to derive their full meaning. It is in that series of statements that Paul introduces the obscure word used throughout the New Testament text as the key word for the love of God, the decision-event love.

> If I speak in the tongues of men and of angels, but have not love [*agapē*], I am a noisy gong or a clanging cymbal. And if I have prophetic powers, and understand all mysteries and all knowledge, and if I have all faith, so as to remove mountains, but have not love [*agapē*], I am nothing. If I give away all I have, and if I deliver my body to be burned, but have not love [*agapē*], I gain nothing (1 Cor. 13:1–3).

Can you see how Paul is stirring up interest in this word? Whatever this word *agapē* describes, it is greater than prophetic powers, greater than the understanding of mysteries—and virtues such as these for the first-century Greek world were terribly high on the value scale. Whatever *agapē* refers to is greater than all knowledge, greater than even the most dynamic kind of faith. Paul boldly states that outside the encompassing context of *agapē*, all these highly acclaimed virtues are incomplete.

Perhaps a contemporary illustration would be appropriate at this point. Berkeley, especially in the spring, is a windy place, and on any afternoon in March or April kites of every description and size can be seen flying from almost every open space, especially along the waterfront. Kites fascinate me. I've thought a lot about them.

Suppose, for a moment, that a kite has a personality of its own, that it has the ability to think and wonder about itself. Suppose that as it flies in the afternoon sky, it feels the surge of wind, the exhilaration of soaring flight, and the continuous, annoying tugging of the string at its center.

Doesn't it seem logical that the kite might say to itself, "If only I could break free from this string that holds me back, then I could really fly"? The reasoning seems sound enough because the string is pulling hard against the kite and is apparently limiting its full freedom. But any boy or girl who has ever flown a kite knows that were the string to break, the kite would not soar freely. Instead it would flutter briefly and then, quite unceremoniously, come crashing to the ground. It is precisely the taut line between the kite and the one who is holding it that enables the kite to fly at all. The tension is good. It is more than good; it is absolutely necessary. Certainly it puts the kite under strain. But it is the very means by which the kite accomplishes what it was designed to do.

In this powerful 13th chapter of 1 Corinthians, Paul sees agape [3] as performing somewhat the same function as a kite string. The tension of the string enables a kite to get off the ground and to soar to its greatest height, to achieve its destiny, so to speak. It allows all the principles of aerodynamics to come into play. So agape love holds us on a true course. It keeps our perspective clear. It gives us a way of viewing the world and our role in it. It brings all the parts of our lives together into an integrated wholeness. Agape is the most crucial of the great strands—faith, hope, and love—in the cord which ties us to God.

Paul speaks of agape as a taut line against the soaring spiritual qualities that for so long had been held in high esteem: mystical speech, prophetic powers, understanding of the deep things of life, even the powerful faith that moves mountains. What he is saying is clear. Think of the kite. Pull out the scissors and cut the cord and, though the display may be impressive for a few moments, the end result will be a broken and chaotic pile of paper and sticks on the ground. To the Christians in Corinth Paul makes this simple point. Take away agape love and every gift, every power, every ethical act, every celebrated quality will crumple and fall in an insignificant heap. Mystical sounds become noise and the knowledge of the angels becomes empty.

Paul has done two important things here. He has, first of all, dared to suggest that these virtues which he has listed are not as ultimately significant as people had been led to believe. They must derive their meaning from something greater. They require still another more essential ingredient than they themselves are able to supply. And then, also, Paul has certainly, and evidently by intention, created interest on the reader's part in finding out what the nature of this other important ingredient is.

In this paragraph Paul calls into question the whole range of human virtues known to the first-century world. Think of how he must have offended the citizens of Corinth! He writes a letter to people whose city god is

Aphrodite, the goddess of love, and strikes at the heart of eros, the kind of love they hold in highest esteem. Even the sensational, "ultimate" experience, the experience of mystical breakthroughs is empty without agape. It signifies absolutely nothing. Prophetic powers, too, and wisdom and understanding without agape are meaningless. Then Paul moves into the faith vocabulary, and finally into the sacrifice vocabulary. Still, he maintains that without this new kind of love, this agape love of the gospel, all of these other virtues, alone or in combination, add up to nothing. Remember the kite. It cannot fly without its cord and someone to hold that cord taut.

Let's take a look back once more at philia and eros. Why aren't these sufficient of themselves? Should we not expect that they would be? Vast numbers of people in all centuries have surely lived out their lives as though they were. What more could a person want than love of family or the love of things beautiful and exciting? Shouldn't the qualities embodied in these existing kinds of love go a long way toward making complete, exciting, fulfilled people? Paul dares to say that they are not enough. Perhaps this then is the place where we should begin to examine the inadequacies of philia and eros.

First, both philia and eros are inadequate foundations to support our lives because they lack *universality*. The focus of each is too confined. Philia, by nature, favors the in-group, the family, the tribe, the special people with whom we feel an instinctive, natural affinity. So Plato in his *Republic* builds a society on the foundations of this type of love, a society in which it is considered appropriate for a small group of citizens, guardians and philosophers, to feel neither obligation nor guilt toward an immense number of men, women, and children classified as slaves. Plato assigns little significance to their lives. He sees nothing wrong with the idea that a whole mass of subcitizen human beings should, as slaves, support his Republic. With philia as the sole basis for operating our lives, we can live on an island of plenty in an ocean of need without feeling the necessity to respond to that need—at least not as long as *our* family has food on the table and is relatively secure. Philia love, by its nature, lacks universality. It doesn't pretend to apply to all people equally.

If philia love is not universal, eros is even less so. Eros is impressed by the fascinating, the beautiful, the smart. This means for eros ever-tightening circles of interest. Its field is select. It is most interested in whatever is upcoming and fashionable. It loves to focus on angels but loses sight of the poor and the plain and the meager. Eros, like philia, is selectively shortsighted.

Second, both of these loves lack *freedom*. Philia has a tendency to cling too tightly to everything around it in order to preserve and protect the intimate, beloved circle of kinship. When we're concerned only about our family or our group or our race, we neither encourage nor permit very much real freedom in our lives. Smothered by alikeness, philia love does not discover the breakthroughs that come from the risks of freedom.

Eros appears at first glance to provide rich soil to support the growth of freedom. But look more closely at it. By its very nature eros desires to be possessed and dominated by the strong, the powerful, and the beautiful. It desires to have its will swept away. We stay with something wondrous and powerful as long as it floods us with experiences of ecstasy. We submit to it to a point where it cancels out our available options. Eros tends to drive us from one ecstatic experience to another, and, therefore, we find very little of the fresh air of true freedom in that desperate search.

Third, both philia and eros lack *justice*. Philia tends to support causes as long as they favor the family or the clan. That's its overriding concern. We can see, therefore, that the motivation for a just, ethical system is ultimately diluted by this internal concern. Philia love downplays any obligation to the larger social whole because it is basically tribal in its orientation. Consequently, the ethics of philia do not easily stretch further than those who bear some definable connection to the favored group. That's an enormous flaw in philia love. There is simply no compelling urgency for justice toward outsiders.

The same is true of eros. Eros is virtually devoid of ethics because it feels obligation only to that which measures up in terms of beauty or excitement. I believe that many marriages are suffering acutely right now because of this. Marriage just can't survive on eros alone, even though this most intimate of relationships rightly has deep roots in eros. If eros is the only basis for our marriage relationships, then we are likely to feel obligation to our spouses only as long as they are youthful and charming and stimulating and satisfying. Eros ethics are sustained by desire and desirability. If we operate out of a framework of eros, we need be obligated to other people only as long as we feel like it and as long as we enjoy that obligation. In the ethics of eros, the people who enter our lives are continually under pressure to merit our favor.

Finally, philia and eros both lack *durability*. Philia is certainly more durable than eros, but it still is limited by a circle of intimate relationships. When we cling too closely to ourselves, to our children, to our possessions, to our group, then we usually end up with far less than we thought we were preserving. On the other hand, I have personally found it to be true that people who are generous, whose horizons and concerns extend beyond themselves and the boundaries of their immediate situations, are people who are most resilient. They have durability. They have staying power. They are growing, exciting people because of their wider relationships. Those who direct their energies toward the inner circle end up as small and confined people. Since philia tends to shun the freedom risks necessary for growth, the result is a lack of true durability. Surprisingly, the assets we cling to the most tightly always seem to escape us.

The great temple in Jerusalem was the symbol of the tribe; it exemplified permanence. Yet Jesus said that it, too, would pass away and that one great stone would not be left on top of another. How this must have troubled the people! But the prediction was true. Things that at one time seem so secure, so permanent, so durable, have a way of disintegrating and falling apart.

Disintegration happens on a smaller, more personal scale too. It happens with human relationships built solely on philia love. I am sure that if I were to go out on the streets of any community and ask men and women in a public opinion poll what they are living for, the majority would respond that they are living primarily for their families. So many people tell me that the one big thing in their lives is their children. That's well and good, but eventually the ones we build our lives on don't need us as much as they once did. Eventually there's less and less demand for the possessive, preserving love of philia. Relationships built entirely on it have a tendency to gradually fall apart. Philia has nowhere to go beyond the small, special group—and the small, special group finally passes away.

Then, of course, eros especially lacks durability. It is bound to youth and the charm of youthful power. It fears time above all enemies. An eros culture resists time. It tries hard to avoid middle age and is resentful of old age. If we have built our sense of worth primarily on eros, we dare not grow old. If we do, we'll lose everything. So the Playboy/Playgirl approach to life flourishes with its cultic, youthful, sensual orientation. Multimillion-dollar businesses have grown up to sell Western society on the myth that what matters more than anything else is youthfulness. That's the primary means of access to eros love. Eros, by its nature, has little durability; it cannot accept the passing of time. It doesn't age well.

Now let's turn our attention again to biblical love. The witness to this special love runs throughout the entire biblical record, both the Old and New Testaments. It is revealed in creation, in events throughout the life of Israel, in the Law, in the prophets, and in the Psalms. Then, in the New Testament this love is supremely revealed by God's intervention in human history in the person of Jesus Christ. In Bethlehem, at a particular point in human history, God presented us with the visible revelation of this love, the concrete event of his self-disclosure.

Often I have been asked what Christian love is or what the love of God is all about. The best response I can make to questions like these is to simply suggest that the inquirer take a look at Jesus Christ. That's the place to look because he *is* that love. That love is clearly spelled out for us in his life, and it is ultimately confirmed for us in his death and resurrection. All agape love in the New Testament gets its definition from him. Jesus *is* the decision-event love of God.

Listen again to Paul as he continues his explanation of agape love in 1 Corinthians 13:4–10:

Love [*agapē*] is patient and kind; love [*agapē*] is not jealous or boastful; it is not arrogant or rude. Love [*agapē*] does not insist on its own way; it is not irritable or resentful; it does not rejoice at wrong, but rejoices in the right. Love [*agapē*] bears all things, believes all things, hopes all things, endures all things.

Love [*agapē*] never ends; as for prophecy, it will pass away; as for tongues, they will cease; as for knowledge, it will pass away. For our knowledge is imperfect and our prophecy is imperfect; but when the perfect comes, the imperfect will pass away.

Paul steadily drives home his point. These other virtues, these other loves of our lives, obviously have their own particular merits, but every one of them needs something more. Agape is that "something more." Look closely at Paul's listing of the attributes of agape. There's the universality that was missing! There's the durability! There's the freedom and the justice!

Paul seems to have no intention of destroying other virtues or of even downplaying them. Understanding, knowledge, prophecy, courage, faith: these are substantial in their own right. God does not intend to steal them away from us. Agape love fulfills them. It provides a context where they can find their proper place. And so it is with philia and eros, those other loves. Agape love enriches our family ties, our national ties, our ethnic ties. Agape love makes us more sensitive to the wonder of the world around us and to the various people who enter our lives. Agape love even makes us more intimate with those in the very inner circle. Agape makes us better lovers. Its fundamental acceptance of the person next to us enriches eros. It completes beauty and intimacy. Agape love, since it originates from and flows out of God's character, enjoys the world because it knows the world's maker.

Paul moves on in this passage to show how his own personal journey with agape has enabled him to be a growing person. He portrays the meaning of maturity in the relational language of his own growing discovery of the character of God and of his own increasing self-understanding.

When I was a child, I spoke like a child, I thought like a child, I reasoned like a child; when I became a man, I gave up childish ways. For now we see in a mirror dimly, but then face to face. Now I know in part; then I shall understand fully, even as I have been fully understood (1 Cor. 13:11–12).

It is agape love that has enabled Paul to make this twofold discovery. He has gained some profound insights into God's nature and into his own as well. His journey with agape is what enabled the fulfillment of the very qualities that the great text opened with—mystical speech, insight, knowledge.

Finally Paul says to the Corinthian Christians: "So faith, hope, love abide, these three; but the greatest of these is love" (1 Cor. 13:13). Love stands out above all the others because it alone is God's decision-event.

-4-

Broken Barriers

R obert Frost's poem "Mending Wall" begins, "Something there is that doesn't love a wall, That wants it down." [1]

Agape love is like that. It's that powerful "something" against all walls, barriers, boundaries—high or low—especially those that wall us in and others out.

Agape, the love revealed in Jesus Christ, doesn't belong exclusively to any group of people or any place or any period of time. It supersedes them all. This love is not more appropriate for one nation or race or political party or social set than any other. It doesn't conform to any of the categories we so readily construct for such things. It just won't stay put. It keeps breaking out of the frameworks that we establish to manage or control it. It's too universal in scope to be confined or controlled.

The brief years of Jesus' earthly ministry were unconventional and full of breakthrough surprises. For one thing, he was always involved with walled-out people such as publicans and sinners. Throughout his entire ministry he refused to be trapped into walled-in confinements of his generation whether it was Jewish nationalism, Sadducee respectability, or Zealot radicalism. Both his disciples and the people at large seemed never prepared emotionally, psychologically, or spiritually for what Jesus offered them.

He offered them a fulfillment beyond the categories they had built up in their minds.

Even during the last encounter of Jesus with his disciples, recorded in Acts 1, the disciples still asked Jesus when he planned to restore the kingdom of Israel. But Jesus had no intention of setting up an earthly kingdom of Israel. Instead, Israel had been brought into a vastly larger Kingdom. Israel was to find its unique significance as a vital part of his Kingdom, and in his Kingdom there is no distinction between Jew or Greek, free man or slave, rich or poor, male or female. It's a much more encompassing Kingdom than anybody, even the disciples, was prepared for. Ancient barriers are down. There are no man-made obstructions to his love. Its scope is limitless! Universal!

A vital concern runs throughout the Book of Acts. Almost all of Jesus' followers seemed to be wrestling with it. Does a person have to become a Jew in order to be a Christian? Put another way: how does a Gentile become a Christian? The first Ecumenical Council of the Church answered questions like these in the context of God's universal intention. Luke records the Council's decision:

> The apostles and the elders were gathered together to consider this matter. And after there had been much debate, Peter rose and said to them, "Brethren, you know that in the early days God made choice among you, that by my mouth the Gentiles should hear the word of the gospel and believe. And God who knows the heart bore witness to them, giving them the Holy Spirit just as he did to us; and he made no distinction between us and them, but cleansed their hearts by faith. Now therefore

why do you make trial of God by putting a yoke upon the neck of the disciples which neither our fathers nor we have been able to bear? But we believe that we shall be saved through the grace of the Lord Jesus, just as they will" (Acts 15:6–11).

That Council contended that the inclusion of the Gentiles into the Commonwealth of God was no hasty afterthought. Instead, it is part of God's original plan which existed from before the foundation of the world. God's love has had a universal intention at its heart from the very beginnings.

The New Testament affirms the universality of God's love in many different ways. Peter, on the one hand, puts it in a very simple and straightforward manner: "Truly I perceive that God shows no partiality, but in every nation any one who fears him and does what is right is acceptable to him" (Acts 10:34–35). Paul, on the other hand, elaborates on the idea with more theological complexity:

> But now in Christ Jesus you who once were far off have been brought near in the blood of Christ. For he is our peace, who has made us both one, and has broken down the dividing wall of hostility, by abolishing in his flesh the law of commandments and ordinances, that he might create in himself one new man in place of the two, so making peace, and might reconcile us both to God in one body through the cross, thereby bringing the hostility to an end. And he came and preached peace to you who were far off and peace to those who were near; for through him we both have access in one Spirit to the Father. So then you are no longer strangers and sojourners, but you are fellow citizens with the saints and members of the household of God (Eph. 2:13–19).

And look at John's vision of heaven in the Book of Revelation (5:9–10). It brings the New Testament teaching about this aspect of God's love to an exciting climax in a chorus of praise:

> . . . and they sang a new song, saying
> "Worthy art thou to take the scroll and to open its seals,
> for thou wast slain and by thy blood didst ransom men for God
> from every tribe and tongue and people and nation, and hast made them a kingdom and priests to our God,
> and they shall reign on earth."

When we respond to God's love in Jesus Christ, the categories that make us distinctive and unique individuals take on new meaning. Our Jewish background or our Chicano background or our Asian background becomes more meaningful. So does our masculinity or our femininity. So do all the other social, economic, political, ethnic categories of our lives. The love of God honors these unique marks of our "createdness" and, at the same time, transcends them.

God endorses our personal worth in two distinct ways. Because of his love, he created us in the first place. That's the basis of the doctrine of Creation. And because of his love he restored us to himself. That's the basis of the doctrine of Redemption. As we come to understand God's redemptive act, we discover that his love grants to us a worth where the emphasis is shifted away from our separateness toward the wholeness we have in Jesus Christ's forgiveness of us all. In that wholeness Christ's love has found us behind each barrier. Therefore, from that central event forward the fences of race, social contrast, even of guilt, have been broken down.

Actually, from the very beginning of the biblical record God has been speaking in universal terms. He promises, for example, that through Abraham's children all the people of the world, not just those in Israel, would be blessed. Throughout the long hard years of occupation and oppression that mark Israel's history, the prophets repeatedly affirm the worldwide scope of God's love and purpose. To be sure, it is not always an easy or welcome theme for them. We find Jonah, for instance, rejecting God's love decision toward the Assyrian capital, the capital of the dreaded enemy of his people. But woven into the entire history of the Hebrew people, with all its ups and downs, is the strong thread: God's love is universally relevant.

The all-encompassing scope of God's love becomes not only an affirmation of the prophets but a daily fact in the ministry of Jesus. The words and the actions of Jesus leave no room for confusion on this point. Whoever has ears to hear may respond to God's love, whether they are Pharisees like Nicodemus (John 3) or publicans like Zacchaeus (Luke 19) or a Syrophoenician woman (Matt. 15) or a Roman official worried about his son's illness (John 4). The traditional confinements of philia and eros are overturned. Jesus touches those with leprosy; he welcomes prostitutes and tax collectors as well as high government officials. He is history's only Man for All Seasons.

Agape love is for everyone. And those who respond be-

come united by that love into a worldwide body, a family
—the Christian church. The church is an inevitable con-
clusion of God's universal intention. Paul elaborates on
this in his letter to the Galatian Christians (3:26–29):

> for in Christ Jesus you are all sons of God, through
> faith. For as many of you as were baptised into Christ
> have put on Christ. There is neither Jew nor Greek,
> there is neither slave nor free, there is neither male nor
> female; for you are all one in Christ Jesus. And if you
> are Christ's then you are Abraham's offspring, heirs ac-
> cording to the promise.

One thing for certain that attests to his love at work in
human life is the crosscultural nature of the Christian
church. What a mixed bag it is! People of every conceiv-
able background and color and position and age and
capacity are drawn together into one single fellowship.
The church of Jesus Christ is a living example of the
sweep of agape love. When we in the church deny or
suppress this universal character of agape we disobey the
very inner force of the Good News itself.

It is Jesus Christ who draws the church into existence.
We are Christians by invitation only—his invitation. As
men and women are convinced by the Holy Spirit of
Christ's love for them as individuals, the Christian church
takes concrete form. The church is real people in real
places invited to each other because of the grace of Christ
which found them. It has been that way from the start.

Look at the church in first-century Corinth, for example. We find evidence in the Corinthian letters and in
Acts 18 that in that particular church were people of all

sorts—women and men, old and young, slaves and free citizens, rich and poor. The church has always been composed of people who often seem to have very little in common except for the fact that Jesus Christ has won each of them to himself. Wherever the gospel is being affirmed, the church becomes this kind of crazy-quilt collection of people—pulled together from various locations and dissimilar situations by his love.

Now let's consider for a moment God's universal love as it is perceived personally. One of the important questions concerning Christian faith is this: how do we discover the reality of God so that we are able to believe— individually and personally? How do the pieces come together enough so that we are able to respond honestly to the truth that God exists and that we ourselves are included in his universal intention? This is the universal question seen in existential, intensely personal terms. Put in its most intimate form: Does God's love include *me*? If it does, then how can *I* know it?

Blaise Pascal developed his own reflections on this question. Pascal observed that there are three major sources of faith: custom, reason, and inspiration. By *custom* he means the witness we receive from the experience of other men and women, both contemporary and historical. The traditions and lives of people around us and of those who have lived before us affirm to our lives the credibility of the Christian gospel. *Reason,* as Pascal sees it, is the internal weighing and questioning of the truthfulness of it all, reasoning that we must do for ourselves, the kind of thing no one else should ever attempt to do for us. We, individually, must struggle to line up the affirmation of the Scripture and the church alongside our own doubts and fears and confusion and the credibility of all other possible options. *Inspiration* is the mysterious self-confirmation by which God himself is his own authentication. Here Pascal points to the ministry of the Holy Spirit which assures us of the authority, the reality, and the love of God's Speech —Jesus Christ.

> The Christian religion, which alone has reason, does not acknowledge as her true children those who believe without inspiration. It is not that she excludes reason and custom. On the contrary, the mind must be opened to proofs, must be confirmed by custom, and offer itself in humbleness to inspirations, which alone can produce a true and saving effect.[2]

As these three sources of faith converge, we are able to believe, to make a meaningful choice. If God's love were solely philia, then custom would be enough for us. What more proof would we need than the warm endorsement of the family or tribe or nation? And were God's love eros, then inspiration alone would be sufficient. There would be no purpose in our weighing the evidence since the involvement of reason and logical thinking is foreign to eros.

The encounter with agape love draws together these three ingredients of faith and, in a dynamic way, the breakthrough takes place. We become convinced not only of God's existence but also of his love. "These things," says Jesus, "I have spoken to you, while I am still with you. But the Counselor, the Holy Spirit, whom the Father will send in my name, he will teach you . . ." (John

14:25-26). Holy Spirit language in the New Testament is companionship language, the language of intimate communication. It is love language. The New Testament writers expect and believe that God himself must, in the long run, be his own proof. Yet, at the same time, they seem fully aware of the dynamics of human response to his love, a response which includes our reason and the witness of custom.

We human beings have a tendency to put things into pigeon holes, to attach labels, to build boxes, and to shape almost anything to fit into the categories we construct. And, in the same way, we have a strong tendency to build protective walls and fences around our lives or parts of our lives to ward off the unexpected—the intruder. God's love, by its very nature, cannot be confined. And it remains universally relevant in spite of all the barriers that we may set against it. That love has reached across the insurmountable barrier between God's truth and our incompleteness in order to find us and to make real to our senses and our intellect his character.

Perhaps the most formidable, awesome barriers in the whole created order are those that surround our inner selves—our personalities. In the deepest sense only love is able to find the hidden doors and passageways through those barriers. Only love is able to work on the complex set of questions, fears, failures, wounds, and dreams that lie in each of us. It is only as we discover and respond to the love of God in Jesus Christ that we are able genuinely to open up ourselves—to let down some of our protective barriers—to be ourselves—to relax in his love.

-5-

The Freedom
That Matters

When Lucy Barfield returns to Narnia and meets the great lion Aslan, in C. S. Lewis's *Prince Caspian*, she immediately expresses her surprise. "Aslan, you're bigger."

"That is because you are older, little one," he answers.

"Not because you are?"

"I am not," the lion replies. "But every year you grow, you will find me bigger." [1]

Agape love has just that kind of expansive effect upon the lives of those who experience it. That's because freedom is one of its essential parts. Agape is free to be free. Other kinds of love have more restraints and are themselves more restraining. Philia, for instance, has no real freedom because it holds on too tightly. It has a tendency to act as a preservative, to protect, to maintain, and when this becomes the main objective in our lives, we find little freedom, little risk. But the love that Jesus Christ reveals, the love that he offers, the love that comes into our lives when we are obedient to him—this is the love that liberates us and continues to do so over the long pull of our lives.

Agape love is able to free us because it itself is free from any bondage or restraints. Agape love, as the New Testament describes it, is born out of the decision God himself makes. His decision to love us is itself free *from* us.

Notice what Paul writes to the Roman Christians: "While we were yet helpless, at the right time Christ died for the ungodly. Why, one will hardly die for a righteous man—though perhaps for a good man one will dare even to die. But God shows his love for us in that while we were yet sinners Christ died for us" (5:6–8). John says it too, "In this is love, not that we loved God but that he loved us" (1 John 4:10). And a little further on in his letter he reemphasizes the point: "We love, because he first loved us" (1 John 4:19).

We do not create God's love, nor do we have any claim to it by virtue of our goodness. It is out of his own freedom that he loves. In other words, the love of God is free at its origin. It existed in the beginning, before we were brought into being, and therefore is shaped only by the character and nature of God himself. The first chapter of Genesis and the first chapter of the Gospel of John bear explicit witness to this fact. God made his own decision about us quite apart from us.

Paul emphasizes something else too. The love of God comes to us even though we are imperfect and sinful. It is imperative that we understand this point. If we believe that we are loved by God because we have earned his love by some virtue of our own, then all our lives we will stand on uncertain ground. We will be continually haunted by a fear that when God discovers the real truth about us, he will stop loving us. To the contrary, the New Testament is consistent on this point: God loves of his own volition, independent of how good or bad we are. He plainly and simply decided to love us. This is the amazing grace about which John Newton wrote his hymn. This is the heart of the good news of the gospel.

The agape love of God, since it is itself free, is able to act as a freeing agent. In his own freedom, by his own sovereign choice, God grants freedom to men and women. Let me put it this way: since agape love originates in God's freedom, that love calls us to freedom too. Agape love, for instance, leaves us free to decide whether or not to receive his love in the first place, whether or not to wager on his love. And then, if we do choose to receive his love, the impact of that love continues to endorse our freedom all the rest of our lives. "Believe in God," says Jesus, "believe also in me" (John 14:1). There's no coercion in a statement like that. It is part of the freedom language of Jesus.

Those two great biblical realities, faith and hope, seem to come into the picture at this point. What is Christian faith? Faith is, simply, our wager on God's love. Christian faith occurs when we step out and trust the love that God offers us. And what is Christian hope? It is actively trusting that God will continue to love us in the future as he has loved us in the past. God allows us many options for our lives. Among other things, he gives us the chance to make a long-term wager of our lives on his love. As we respond positively to his offer, we find that the liberating effect of his love increases and strengthens our faith and our hope.

This new kind of love will free us to move into new areas of living. Jesus discusses some of the practical implications of agape love in the Sermon on the Mount. "You have heard that it was said, 'You shall love your neighbor and hate your enemy.' But I say to you, Love your enemies and pray for those who persecute you" (Matt. 5:43–44). Jesus calls us to be free from our past prejudices and patterns. He sets a course for his followers that is obviously new and even dangerous. He pushes back our horizons.

Dietrich Bonhoeffer writes of this very thing from a Nazi prison camp. "I notice repeatedly here how few there are who can harbour conflicting emotions at the same time. When bombers come, they are all fear; when there is something nice to eat, they are all greed. . . . By contrast, Christianity puts us into many different dimensions of life at the same time." [2]

Look at the freedom we have in this new kind of love! Now, for instance, we have an alternative to the old reciprocity cycle: we are wronged by someone; we respond in like manner. What's new or original about that? But the kind of love that Jesus offers introduces a genuinely new reality into the picture. It breaks open the old containers of our lives. And with these new dimensions of living Jesus promises companionship with himself to make it all work. Love those who reject and persecute us? Agape provides the freedom to become a part of that new love. "This is my commandment," says Jesus, "that you love one another as I have loved you" (John 15:12).

Luke gives us a glimpse of the freedom aspect of agape as he relates an incident in the life of one particular person, Zacchaeus, a collector of taxes.

He entered Jericho and was passing through. And there was a man named Zacchaeus; he was a chief tax collector, and rich. And he sought to see who Jesus was, but could not, on account of the crowd, because he was small of stature. So he ran on ahead and climbed up into a sycamore tree to see him, for he was to pass that way. And when Jesus came to the place, he looked up and said to him, "Zacchaeus, make haste and come down; for I must stay at your house today." So he made haste and came down, and received him joyfully. And when they saw it they all murmured, "He has gone in to be the guest of a man who is a sinner." And Zacchaeus stood and said to the Lord, "Behold, Lord, the half of my goods I give to the poor; and if I have defrauded any one of anything, I restore it fourfold." And Jesus said to him, "Today salvation has come to this house . . ." (Luke 19:1–9).

Here is a graphic illustration of the liberating effect of one man's discovery of the love of Jesus Christ. Zacchaeus accepts Jesus into his house, into his life, and in the process is freed ethically to act out in concrete ways the love he has experienced from Jesus Christ. He is set free to repent of his exploitation of the people as a tax collector and is motivated to begin repayment to those whom he has wronged. Salvation has, indeed, come to his house.

Salvation always results in real freedom. In fact Paul describes salvation as freedom in his letter to the Galatians. Salvation literally means being set free from death, and that is the essence of Jesus' resurrection. In Christ, through his love, we have been freed from death—we don't have to fear it any longer. We are set free from fear. John says that perfect love removes fear (1 John 4:18). We no longer need be enslaved to our fears or our failures, our mistakes or our bad choices or the future or anything. We are free! We are even free from other people around us. They don't control the meaning of our lives any longer. We are free from all the things we once hung on to, to make our lives meaningful and worthwhile. Jesus Christ, by his making us safe, by his love, sets us truly free.

He also sets us free to do certain things, to act in certain ways. From the Christian point of view, the greatest proof of freedom comes, paradoxically, when we are enabled to obligate ourselves to others. That's real freedom because we must feel genuinely secure and in touch with ourselves before we can give ourselves away to others. We must have personally experienced love before we can share it. When we always have to hedge on every decision we make, we don't have true freedom. Instead, that's a sign of bondage. But when we can freely give ourselves to others without worries or constraints, without having to plan for possible retreat, that is freedom fully experienced. Only agape love liberates us like that. Only agape love frees us from ourselves enough to allow us to act responsibly toward others regardless of their ties to us.

Again Dietrich Bonhoeffer catches the significance of the freedom in agape.

> Christ kept himself from suffering till his hour had come, but when it did come he met it as a free man, seized it, and mastered it. Christ, so the Scriptures tell us, bore the sufferings of all humanity in his own body as if they were his own—a thought beyond our comprehension—accepting them of his own free will. . . .

We are not Christ, but if we want to be Christians, we must have some share in Christ's large-heartedness by acting with responsibility and in freedom when the hour of danger comes, and by showing a real sympathy that springs, not from fear, but from the liberating and redeeming love of Christ for all who suffer. Mere waiting and looking on is not Christian behaviour. The Christian is called to sympathy and action, not in the first place by his own sufferings, but by the sufferings of his brethren, for whose sake Christ suffered.[3]

-6-

Rightness, Wrongness, and Redemption

In describing the scope and force of agape, Paul explains, "It does not rejoice at wrong, but rejoices in the right" (1 Cor. 13:7).

What makes agape good and honest? What about it is just and righteous? Why can it be called true? As I see it, two ingredients are involved in Paul's affirmation. One is an ethical or truth ingredient—the part that is concerned with what is right and wrong and true. But within this context of justice and righteousness there is a second element—the redemption ingredient, the care ingredient.

Agape, as Paul says, rejoices not in wrongdoing but in doing right. This means that agape love is not afraid of facing up to human sin. Herein lies a salient feature of agape—a characteristic that makes it radically different from other kinds of love. Eros cannot face up to the seamy side of the human situation because it has its focus in another, quite opposite, place. The Greeks thought of religious love in the beauty terms of eros. Eros just isn't comprehensive enough to encompass some things—things like injustice and tragedy. Philia love has this same general problem though not in as narrow a sense. It is not able to grapple with the wide-ranging implications of moral tragedy either. Often philia will even seek to cover up sin. Its protective, preserving nature causes it to have a strong tendency to cover, overlook, ignore, or hide unpleasant things or unjust situations, rather than run the risk of giving the individual or the family or the intimate group a bad name. This means that philia has, because of its nature, a strong desire to downplay human weakness and tragedy rather than face it and work it through.

New Testament love is not afraid to face up to tragedy. This fact is superbly illustrated in Malcolm Muggeridge's book *Something Beautiful for God*, the story of Mother Teresa of Calcutta. Muggeridge went to Calcutta as a correspondent for the *Times* of London to do a newspaper story about this remarkable Albanian sister and her Home for Dying Destitutes. While there, he discovered a quality of life and love that deeply moved him. Its power was evident. It had a radiance, a shine, an ethical clarity about it that he describes as "something beautiful." He was so impressed with what he saw that he ended up writing a book about these Roman Catholic missionaries and their work.

Mother Teresa's conviction is that men and women should at least be able to die in the presence of a person who cares. So she and her fellow workers began their ministry by going every day into the streets of Calcutta and taking the dying poor off the streets into a small house which they maintained. This small band of women first took in their fellow human beings to offer them assistance and the love of Christ in their last days. Then they began to expand their work through the Sisters of Charity to outcasts of all types, especially to orphan children.

Muggeridge compares her approach to people in need with his own response:

> I was being driven one evening in my car when my driver knocked someone over—something as easily done then as now, with the crowded pavements spilling over into the roadway. With great resourcefulness, and knowing the brawls that could so easily develop when a European car was involved in a street accident, my driver jumped out, grabbed the injured man, put him in the driving seat beside him, and drove away at top speed to the nearest hospital. There, I rather self-righteously insisted on seeing that the man was properly attended to (as it turned out, he was not seriously hurt), and, being a sahib, was able to follow him into the emergency ward. It was a scene of inconceivable confusion and horror, with patients stretched out on the floor, in the corridors, everywhere. While I was waiting, a man was brought in who had just cut his throat from ear to ear. It was too much; I made off, back to my comfortable flat and a stiff whisky and soda, to expatiate through the years to come on Bengal's wretched social conditions, and what a scandal it was, and how it was greatly to be hoped that the competent authorities would . . . and so on . . .
>
> I ran away and stayed away; Mother Teresa moved in and stayed. That was the difference.[1]

That's the difference! That's the difference between agape and eros. That's also the difference between agape and philia. That's the sort of difference agape love makes. Agape love moves into a tough situation and stays. Agape love has justice, righteousness, and truth in it. It is not frightened off by the worst kind of human sin or need; it is not afraid of the deepest of human crises. The tragedies with which Mother Teresa must cope in Calcutta and in the other places into which she has expanded her work are wholescale human tragedies. They astound our senses. They are so enormous and seemingly so hopeless.

But, says Muggeridge, there she was,

> . . . rather slightly built, with a few rupees in her pocket; not particularly clever, or particularly gifted in the arts of persuasion. Just with this Christian love shining about her; in her heart and on her lips. Just prepared to follow her Lord . . .
>
> I never experienced so perfect a sense of human equality as with Mother Teresa among her poor. Her love for them, reflecting God's love, makes them equal, as brothers and sisters within a family are equal, however widely they differ in intellectual and other attainments, in physical beauty and grace.[2]

So Mother Teresa moves in to the middle of this heartbreaking human situation and stays. Because of agape! To her, every human life has worth because of the prior fact of God's decision to love. The worth of every single individual, no matter how destitute or tragic, has already been established by God, and Mother Teresa sees this!

What is there about agape that makes it able to face up to such calamity? What enables it to deal with human situations as they actually are without recourse to fantasy or sentimentality? It's because agape is *reality oriented*. It faces up to the real thing without resorting to escapism. So we have the agape love of the New Testament facing up, for example, to the mixed needs and problems of the disciples, helping each of them see who he really is with the insight that agape provides.

One of my colleagues in the ministry, James Angell, makes this perceptive observation about the nature of agape in his book *Yes Is a World:*

> The demand to be loved is unrelenting. When that need is frustrated we will use every device we know to gain it, or we pay for the lack of it in fear, depression, or rage. In Western culture a person and his performance tend to merge. We are supposed to deserve love, or qualify for it by correct behavior; when that doesn't happen and we go unloved, we make these psychological retaliations.
>
> Agape love . . . knows how to love even when performance is bad.[3]

"Do you love me?" Jesus asks Peter by the Lake of Galilee following the resurrection. In fact, he repeats that same present-tense question three times in succession. "Do you love me?" "Feed my sheep," Jesus instructs him when he says he does. Only as Peter grapples with his answer to Jesus' question is he able to discover who he really is, and only in the repeated imperative following his answer is Peter able to understand the completeness of Christ's acceptance of him. (See John 21:15–19.)

What is it about Christian love that makes it able to stay and get to work on our crises, our sins, and our ethical problems? Agape love is able to come face to face with both the victims of sin and the perpetrators of sin because it sees a way through. It sees a way through human sin and human need because it believes in repentance and in redemption. That is why it can be reality oriented. That is why it doesn't have to run away from tragedy.

Dostoevski's *Crime and Punishment* provides a classic example of the ethics of agape. Raskolnikov, the young student, commits a terrible crime. He murders two people for their money. He rationalizes his crime in several ways: Napoleon, he tells himself, murdered thousands and became a hero; the two people he murdered were only miserly, insignificant people; he would use the money to advance his career for the good of mankind.

Most of this great novel, however, deals with the punishment, not the crime. Raskolnikov's punishment comes from many directions. Another person even confesses to the crime, so Raskolnikov theoretically is no longer suspect. The police, at least officially, aren't looking for the murderer any more. Raskolnikov should feel good, but he doesn't. His body is racked with physical suffering and his spiritual and emotional natures are battling. The punishment begins to grind away at his life—from the inside.

Two other very important characters appear in this novel. One is the detective Petrovich who, not believing the confession of the other man, continues to hunt Raskolnikov down, but never succeeds in catching him. The other is Sonia, a young girl who loves Raskolnikov. Look closely at the nature of Sonia's love, for in many ways it is a replica of the love of Jesus Christ. Sonia's is an unusual kind of love. At first glance, you might not even recognize it as love. Sonia's love for Raskolnikov, first of all, drives him to confess that he is the murderer. At one point, after she discovers that he has, in fact, killed those two people, she tells him that he must go out into the center of town and kiss the earth because he has defiled it with the blood of two innocent human beings. She even tells him that he must cry to the north, south, east, and west that he is a murderer. It is her love that compels him to make that confession.

That's what agape love does. It meets a crisis head on. As Mother Teresa faced up to the crisis on the streets of Calcutta, so the love of Sonia faces up to the tragic situation of this young man Raskolnikov without any sort of evasion. When Jesus causes us to take a look at ourselves in the New Testament, when he confronts us with the implications of our sins, when he reveals to us the extent of our guilt to the point that we must face up to our need for repentance—that is love. Believe me, that is the deepest kind of love. It's not theoretical or fanciful. It's concrete. It exposes us. Sonia, the one who loves Raskolnikov, is the one who talks him into confessing that he is the murderer. So Raskolnikov is convicted and sent off to Siberia. Sonia won. The detective won. That's love.

You may be thinking, "Well, if that's love, I don't particularly think I want any part of it." But continue on. Love doesn't end there. When Raskolnikov is sent off to a Siberian prison, suffering from tuberculosis and pneumonia, Petrovich, the detective who represents the law, says his farewell and immediately turns his attention to other criminals. He is interested solely in justice, and, for him, justice has been done. But not for Sonia. Sonia follows Raskolnikov over all the hard miles to Siberia. She almost dies. By foraging potatoes or cabbages or anything she can find, she keeps herself and the young man alive throughout his long nine-year sentence. That's agape love in action. That's love with both justice and redemption in it. Love follows through to the place where salvation occurs in spite of the tragedy.

Malcolm Muggeridge gets at this when he emphasizes how Mother Teresa came to Calcutta and stayed. Muggeridge saw the hospital, and his response was to go back to comfortable surroundings in England and write about his experience as his righteous indignation boiled over. But, Mother Teresa stayed right there. This is an essential contrast. Sonia goes all the way to Siberia. Her love not only believes and rejoices in the right but believes there is a kindness in God's justice. It sees through the justice to redemption. In a great final scene in *Crime and Punishment* Raskolnikov receives that forgiveness and experiences a resurrection of new life.

Agape love is not willing to settle merely for justice as Petrovich did, nor is it willing to settle merely for the accurate identification of problems as Muggeridge at first found himself doing. Its concern is not only for truth, but for people. Only agape love sees us through the truth crisis all the way to the redemption solution.

Muggeridge makes a further observation about the work of Mother Teresa's Sisters of Charity. "It's perfectly true, of course," he comments, "that, statistically speaking, what she achieves is little, or even negligible." Certainly, in the great sea of human need, Mother Teresa's rescuing a few dying people to give them a few hours of peace at the end of their lives isn't very significant. One Sonia traveling off to Siberia to rescue one person isn't very earthshaking. What we accomplish as agape love moves us to help real people in real need may seem very small, perhaps even irrelevant. Surely it's no match for the staggering need of the times we are in. Statistically all this is perfectly true. But Muggeridge goes on to analyze it himself, "But then Christianity is not a statistical view of life." [4]

I love that sentence! That there should be more joy in heaven over one sinner who repents than over all the hosts of the just is definitely an antistatistical proposition.[5] "Mother Teresa," says Muggeridge, "is fond of saying that welfare is for a purpose—an admirable and a necessary one—whereas Christian love is for a person." [6] Agape love has an instinct for the individual who has been harmed or injured, for the individual person in need, because it is the personal, individual act of God in history. Agape love is just and personal and can face up to anything: unimpressive statistics, even our sins, and we know how unique and personal those can be.

Responding to the love of Jesus Christ should make us more joyful and exhilarated than we have ever felt before. It should make us feel absolutely great. Well, that may or may not be the case. When Jesus Christ touches our lives with his love there is the distinct possibility that he may make us feel more guilty than we ever have before. In his love he will make us feel very uncomfortable with our sins. Agape love will uncover our real nature and will often produce perplexing guilt feelings. But agape love will stay with us in the midst of our guilt through our tough decisions that reach out to God for help, and at last into redemption. For agape love, no situation is irrevocable. There is no situation that cannot be healed. Love has staying power. Agape love is a long-term obligation and a long-term living out of the love of God.

Another view of the ethics of this New Testament love is given us at the beginning of Paul's second letter to the Christians at Corinth. Here, as in 1 Corinthians 13, Paul repeatedly uses one particular word:

> Blessed be the God and Father of our Lord Jesus Christ, the Father of mercies and God of all *comfort,* who *comforts* us in all our affliction, so that we may be able to *comfort* those who are in any affliction, with the *comfort* with which we ourselves are *comforted* by God. For as we share abundantly in Christ's sufferings, so through Christ we share abundantly in *comfort* too. If we are afflicted, it is for your *comfort* and salvation; and if we are *comforted,* it is for your *comfort,* which you experience when you patiently endure the same sufferings that we suffer. Our hope for you is unshaken; for we know that as you share in our sufferings, you will also share in our *comfort* (2 Cor. 1:3–7).

The word that Paul uses over and over (*paraklēsis,* verb *parakaleō*) translated in the Revised Standard Version as *comfort,* literally in the Greek means "to call alongside," and therefore "to walk alongside, to encourage." Read the passage again with that translation: "He comes alongside us in all our affliction, so that we may be able to come alongside those who are in any affliction." That's the kind of love the New Testament proclaims. It's a love that has in it both a concern for truth and a caring concern for individual people. It's a love with both justice and kindness in it. Agape love comes alongside us wherever we are, and, as a result, enables us to come alongside others in a helping relationship.

"The biggest disease today," says Mother Teresa, "is not leprosy or tuberculosis, but rather the feeling of being unwanted, uncared for and deserted by everybody. The greatest evil is the lack of love and charity, the terrible indifference towards one's neighbour who lives at the roadside assaulted by exploitation, corruption, poverty, and disease." [7]

The need for agape love has never been greater. But when we step out into the agape adventure, some unsettling things may happen to us. For one thing, we'll see ourselves much more clearly than we did before. And then we'll see the human situation around us in a completely new light. We will also discover new obligations to our fellow human beings. But along with these new insights into ourselves and along with these new imperatives concerning our world comes a solid offer of the close companionship of Jesus. He offers his love. He offers himself. He offers to live his life through us. All the equipment we need for the new adventure has been amply provided.

"I am with you always, to the close of the age" (Matt. 28:20). Jesus himself said that.

-7-

Love
That Lasts

Remember the queen in Snow White and the Seven Dwarfs? Every day she asks the magic mirror for reassurance, "Mirror, mirror on the wall, who is fairest of them all?" It is inevitable that sooner or later when the queen goes to the mirror, she will learn that someone else in the kingdom is more beautiful than she. When that moment comes, tragedy will strike. Actually, though, the tragedy began for her long before, when she started asking the question. The queen, like so many of us, finds herself caught up in an obsession with eros, and eros characteristically fears time because it doesn't wear well. Because of its preoccupation with beauty and power, eros cannot endure time. People who have structured their lives around eros eventually discover the irreversibility of time. The foundations of eros slowly, relentlessly wear away, and as we come to a realization of what is happening to us, we may panic, or worse, like the queen, seek solutions that hurt those around us.

Even philia, the love of our own bodies and everything that is naturally connected to us, finally runs out. Its durability is far too dependent on the localized structures that we build around us. It doesn't matter so much whether we're talking about a pyramid that an Egyptian pharaoh builds, about financial or family security, or about a respectable job or a distinguished reputation or a beautiful home. All of these things eventually lose their significance with time. They eventually fade away. And with their passing, lives built only on these foundations crumble.

But there is a love that is durable, that is able to stick it out. The New Testament abounds with descriptions of it. Paul tells of his own experiences in his first letter to the Corinthians. "Love bears all things," he says, "believes all things, hopes all things, endures all things" (1 Cor. 13:7). This love has strength and permanence. It also has hope. It allows men and women to have confidence in the future.

Young couples will sometimes tell me that they are afraid to have children in these uneasy times. It may be that we are currently experiencing a measurable decline in our national birth rate because so many in our generation are apprehensive about the future. Christian love, quite to the contrary, wagers on the future. Agape has hope for the future because the future belongs to God. And so Paul can say quite flatly, "Love never ends" (1 Cor. 13:8).

To expand on this point, Paul goes on to say that "as far prophecy, it will pass away; as for tongues, they will cease; as for knowledge, it will pass away. For our knowledge is imperfect and our prophecy is imperfect; but when the perfect comes, the imperfect will pass away" (1 Cor. 13:8–10). The Greek word used here for *perfect* is *teleios* meaning completed, full-grown. The root word *telos* (end or goal) from which we get the first part of our English word *telescope,* is the fulfillment word of the New Testament. Perhaps it will be helpful to think of Paul's promise in this way: eventually what is at the culmination of things will come up close so that we will really see it for ourselves and experience the fulfillment of God's love.

The New Testament gives two reasons why this agape love is so durable. For one thing, its foundations are solid, strong, and ultimate. But more than that, agape is not static. It's alive! Its staying power is not simply founded in its rocklike permanence, but in its ability to grow.

What are the foundations of agape? Perhaps we can best discover them by posing a basic existential question. How can we know we are really, in actual fact, loved? How can we know that those around us, even our enemies, are loved? I've sometimes asked myself this when I have been in a packed crowd at the Oakland Coliseum or at Memorial Stadium on the University of California campus. Can God really intimately know and love every individual in this mass of people? And then my thought process really bogs down when I realize that those surging crowds are but a mere ripple in the vast sea of humanity on the face of the earth. Can God really care about each one of us personally? Intimately? Can each one of us really depend on the love of God for our individual lives?

The New Testament says we can. The primary reason it gives is simply because God says so. "But to all who received him, who believed in his name, he gave the power to become children of God" (John 1:12). Now that affirmation may either impress us or it may sound impossible or trite, depending on where we are coming from in our lives. I've mentioned several times already that agape love is the decision-event love. Look at it from the perspective of the most famous verse in all the Bible, "For God so loved the world that he gave his only Son, that whoever believes in him should not perish but have eternal life" (John 3:16). That's a durability statement. That durability depends entirely on God's decision.

How do we know that we are loved? How do we count on that love for the future? The New Testament response is that we know it and we count on it because God's word and his actions authenticate the promise. God said he loved the world. "For God so loved the world that he gave his only son. . . ." Then John adds a further bold statement, "For God sent the Son into the world, not to condemn the world, but that the world might be saved through him" (John 3:17).

The world, the whole created order, gets its meaning because of the decision God has made, out of which he created the world and by which he redeemed the world. In the mystery of redemption, as you and I elect to receive that redemption, not only are we saved as individuals, but, by our experience of God's grace, the whole world benefits. Paul and John both reflect on this point, and it becomes the culmination of Jesus' prayer for the church in John 17: "I in them and thou in me, that they may become perfectly one, so that the world may know that thou hast sent me and hast loved them even as thou hast loved me" (John 17:23). Through Jesus Christ and his love at work in our lives, the whole created order is blessed.

According to the New Testament, our individual worth

and significance is not at all dependent on the shifting sands of other people's sentiment. That's the problem with philia and eros. Both have an innate dependence on the opinions of others, or on our feelings, or on a combination of these. The New Testament teaches that our worth, our belovedness, is dependent entirely on God's decisive act. God has not only said he loves us and values us, but he has acted it out in history. This is the importance of the physical coming of Jesus Christ into the world. The Word became Event. How can we know that we are loved? God has not only said so over the centuries, but he did something very concrete. He stepped into the world at Christmas and came to live among us and to die for us and, thereby, to conquer death itself for us. There is no more substantial object lesson in love.

One of the practical implications of this is that God's love for us is not swept away because of the grossness of our sins or the sins of others. I've talked with concerned people periodically about the problem of unforgivable sin, people who are wondering if some sin they have committed has irreparably cut them off from the love of God. The sins I have heard about are certainly real, so I can't simply say, "Let's imagine them away." They actually happened, and often other people are paying for them in various ways. So what about unforgivable sin? Is there a possibility that a cumulation of sin or a particular sin can permanently separate us from the love of God? Just how durable is his love in the face of consistent, blatant human wrongdoing?

Think about Peter. He denied Jesus three times on the

night Jesus needed him most. Peter knew firsthand what sin was all about. Among other things, he knew Jesus better than most of us ever will, and yet he repeatedly denied that he knew him. Peter's flat denial certainly makes him a good candidate for a place on the "unforgivable sin" list. Yet look at what happens in Peter's relationship with Christ following the resurrection as Mark records it.

> And entering the tomb, they saw a young man sitting on the right side, dressed in a white robe; and they were amazed. And he said to them, "Do not be amazed; you seek Jesus of Nazareth, who was crucified. He has risen, he is not here; see the place where they laid him. But go, tell his disciples *and Peter* that he is going before you to Galilee; there you will see him, as he told you" (Mark 16:5–7).

And Peter! In those two words, which we can so easily pass over, Mark reveals the powerful durability of the love of God. Christ's love for his disciples is so much more real and lasting than eros or philia. It even outlasts Peter's denial.

Peter is restored to fellowship with Jesus because of the reliability of Christ's love. Jesus Christ's love sticks it out with Peter. Jesus not only heals this relationship with him, but later he goes so far as to restore Peter to a position of central leadership among the disciples. His love wears well.

Here is another fact that attests to the durability of God's love. It does not dissolve in the face of the real distresses of our lives. Maybe we can handle the first implication and say, "All right, we believe that our sins are not able to

cancel out his love. His love will call us to repentance."
But what about the enormous stresses of life and living?
Maybe our concern is not so much about personal sin as
it is about the vast sweep of history where the sense of
tragedy is not only personal but global and social. What
about the natural and the man-made holocausts of history?
How does God's love fit into all of that? How is God's love
able to endure in those situations?

The hymn "Great Is Thy Faithfulness" means a great
deal to my congregation in Berkeley, as it does to many
Christians. That hymn is another durability statement. It
receives its inspiration from a text in Lamentations which
was written by Jeremiah following the fall of his beloved
Jerusalem when all the fortunes of Judah seemed to have
collapsed. Observe the surprising context for this great
statement of confidence and hope:

> I am the man who has seen affliction
>   under the rod of his wrath;
> he has driven and brought me
>   into darkness without any light;
> surely against me he turns his hand
>   again and again the whole day long.
>
> He has made my flesh and my skin waste away,
>   and broken my bones;
> he has besieged and enveloped me
>   with bitterness and tribulation;
> he has made me dwell in darkness
>   like the dead of long ago.
>
> He has walled me about so that I cannot escape;
>   he has put heavy chains on me;

> though I call and cry for help,
>   he shuts out my prayer;
> he has blocked my ways with hewn stones,
>   he has made my path crooked.
>
> He is to me like a bear lying in wait,
>   like a lion in hiding;
> he led me off my way and tore me to pieces;
>   he has made me desolate;
> he bent his bow and set me
>   as a mark for his arrow.
>
> He drove into my heart
>   the arrows of his quiver;
> I have become the laughingstock of all peoples,
>   the burden of their songs all day long.
> He has filled me with bitterness,
>   he has sated me with wormwood.
>
> He has made my teeth grind on gravel,
>   and made me cower in ashes;
> my soul is bereft of peace,
>   I have forgotten what happiness is;
> So I say, "Gone is my glory,
>   and my expectation from the Lord."
>   —Lamentations 3:1–18

Look at Jeremiah! Feel for him as he plumbs the depths of his soul, lamenting, complaining. How heavily the distress of his time weighs upon him. How bad it all is. How hopeless. But listen! He goes on for a sentence or two more:

> Remember my affliction and my bitterness,
>   the wormwood and the gall!

My soul continually thinks of it
   and is bowed down within me.
But this I call to mind,
   and therefore I have hope:

The steadfast love of the Lord never ceases,
   his mercies never come to an end;
They are new every morning;
   great is thy faithfulness.
                —Lamentations 3:19–21

That's the text of a great hymn. It rises out of the ashes of despair. To really understand the hymn we probably should sing the whole of that Lamentation. Jeremiah wasn't trying to grind out lyrics for another popular song for the hymnal. These words emerge from the agony of his heart. His city had fallen. His people had been carried off. His whole life was surrounded by disaster. Everything around him seemed to have collapsed. Yet he called to his memory something that gave him hope—the love of God. Even in the midst of unparalleled stress, it was there for him. Because of it, he could put his trust in God even in bitter times.

People who have suffered greatly have told me that, during times of the deepest pain and bitterness and disappointment, the only thing that provided any sort of solid support was their assurance of the love of God. This portion of Lamentations is a text that many suffering men and women have discovered. It is honest about the suffering and despair. Yet it speaks of a love that lasts.

The other durability feature of agape love is that *it grows*. Agape is the direct result of our day-to-day relationship with Jesus Christ. That is an important thing to understand. Agape love is not an energy or a force that floats through our lives in some mysterious way. It is a personal, close relationship. It is the event—Jesus Christ—alongside us.

Some of what I hear or read on the subject of Christian love disappoints me because it is so vague. Sometimes Christian love is treated as if it were a great ideal to which we should aspire. That view seems basically wrong—it's up there, so high, so lofty, so beautiful that it couldn't possibly be approached, let alone personally experienced, by normal, average men and women who have to live out their lives on the streets of our cities. But that isn't at all what the New Testament teaches. Agape love is not an ideal; it's the result of a growing relationship that can be going on with Jesus Christ right now.

Screwtape, the senior devil in C. S. Lewis's *The Screwtape Letters* through whom Lewis makes some pointed observations on the Christian life, gives a few intriguing suggestions to his subordinate Wormwood—a junior tempter—on how to destroy a person's love. "Do what you will, there is going to be some benevolence, as well as some malice, in your patient's soul. The great thing is to direct the malice to his immediate neighbours whom he meets every day and to thrust his benevolence out to the remote circumference, to people he does not know." [1]

Screwtape goes on to explain that every human life should be thought of in terms of concentric circles: the inner circle being the person's will, his deciding; the next circle his intellect; and the last circle, his fantasy. Screwtape urges Wormwood to keep his patient's love "out there" someplace and not let it get next to someone close like a neighbor's child or a fellow worker. Direct the malice toward the inner circle, he tells Wormwood, and direct the love to the ideal, the fantasy circle. Then the love won't amount to anything, but the malice will be very real.

We dare not turn agape love into some great ideal that's way out there on the distant circumference line. Agape love grows out of our obedience to Jesus Christ, and therefore it works in the inner circles. It works on a day-by-day basis with ups and downs in the middle of real life. We must not idealize the love of God. If we do, we'll never have it in our lives. We can idealize some of the other kinds of love, but agape doesn't fit well in that kind of box. Agape can't be packaged. It's the result of our relationship with Jesus Christ, and that relationship can be very rough and uneven, at times even stormy. But agape love is there even when we forget about it, even when we are disobedient. And when we come back for forgiveness, that love is what heals the situation. It's what enables us to get back up and begin again. It sticks with us even with all our imperfections, and there's no way we'll ever be able to get rid of all those. The love of God isn't a spiritual ideal. It results from a relationship. It's alive. It grows in our lives from day to day. That's why it lasts so well.

As growing individuals we need this growing kind of love. It is not God's will to turn us instantly into completed disciples. Rather, with all our faults and weaknesses, we grow into maturity as God's Spirit works within us. The Holy Spirit helps us with those weaknesses

(Rom. 8:26). This also means that the agape love we extend to others will always be incomplete and uneven. But as we share the love we have received from God, the healing, dynamic effect of that love on our relationships with others will amaze us.

Now, a final consideration. Does agape love rule out all other kinds of love in our lives? It may appear as if I've been pretty hard on philia and eros! But they are not discarded once we've experienced agape. Far from it. As a matter of fact, if we look at the New Testament as a whole, we'll see that, as a result of agape love, the other loves of our lives are made richer. They are enabled to assume their most creative nature. But we shouldn't expect too much from them in isolation. We shouldn't expect to get meaning for living from our families or the color of our skin or how much personal charisma we generate or how many possessions we are able to collect. No. The New Testament explains how to discover meaning for our lives. We receive our meaning directly from God's love. Everything else and everybody else derives meaning from that love too—family ties, the beauty we see around us, and all the other loves of our lives become deeper and richer. It all stems from that ultimate, personal love—agape. Universal. Free. Just. Durable.

-8-

The Agape Experience

J ust what happens when we decide to wager on this decision-event love of the New Testament? If we welcome God's love into our lives, what kind of impact will it make on us? Will the experience overwhelm us? Will God's love totally stun our senses and intellect with its marvel and power? The Bible, you know, often shouts out the greatness and wonder of God's love. Look at Psalm 89:6–8:

> For who in the skies can be compared to the Lord?
>   Who among the heavenly beings is like the Lord,
> a God feared in the council of the holy ones,
>   great and terrible above all that are round about him?
> O Lord God of hosts,
>   who is mighty as thou art, O Lord . . . ?"

The Bible is emphatic about the greatness of God. God's power cannot be rivaled. There are neither princes, nor dominions, nor powers in heaven or on the earth or in hell to match the power, the immensity of God. If therefore, we appropriate this powerful kind of love into our lives, this love that God has decided to offer us, will we be left speechless? Will we be totally dazzled? Melted down? Cancelled out? What exactly happens to a person coming into the presence of such matchless love?

An ideal religious experience for a great many people

would include a sense of being totally swept away by God's grace and power. That's an understandable and logical expectation especially for a person who has been able to comprehend something of the wonder of God and who sees the staggering contrast between our smallness and God's greatness. How could it be otherwise? So it's not hard to see why we often tend to pray for this kind of overwhelming experience. Our prayers often seem to be saying, "Lord, overwhelm us! Lord, astound us with your presence! Lord, cancel out our doubts and our questions! Give us a mystical experience that will so overpower us that we will have no choice but to believe in you!"

Many of us want our relationship with God to be set in a context like this. We want from God elaborate proofs of his spectacular power. We want God to give us special, unmistakable signs of his love. What we are looking for, then, is eros love. This is precisely what the Greeks meant when they spoke of eros in the religious sense. This is the kind of experience they sought in worship. When the first-century Greek mystic prayed to a god or gods, he was primarily seeking to be overcome by the ultimate magnificence of deity and beauty. He wanted to be shattered; he wanted to feel the "high of all highs." This is eros, the love won from us by the sheer beauty and majesty of the loved or worshiped object.

Into this mind-set, this context, came the Love of the New Testament. Into all this stepped Jesus.

Against this background, I think we are better able to understand Jesus' three temptations by Satan in the wilderness. The devil takes Jesus to the pinnacle of Herod's great temple and tries to persuade him to jump from its towering height into the courtyard below, saying that angels would surely rescue him before his feet struck the ground. This spectacular scene obviously would have stunned the senses of the people in the great temple courtyard below. They would have had no choice but to believe in the awesome power of Jesus. Such a clear and unmistakable display of supernatural power would have left no possibility for doubt, at least for that afternoon.

A similar dynamic is involved when Jesus is urged by the devil to turn rocks into bread. Dostoevski wrestles with the implications of that temptation in his novel *The Brothers Karamazov*. As he unfolds the history of the Karamazov family, Dostoevski also paints a vivid picture of the struggle of faith with disbelief, particularly in a poem which one of the brothers writes, The Legend of the Grand Inquisitor. In the poem, the Grand Inquisitor in Spain says to Jesus, who has come to Spain, and has been arrested:

"You wanted to come into the world and You came empty-handed, with nothing but some vague promise of freedom, which, in their simple-mindedness and innate irresponsibility, men cannot even conceive and which they fear and dread, for there has never been anything more difficult for man and for human society to bear than freedom! And now, do You see those stones in this parched and barren desert? Turn them into loaves of bread and men will follow You like cattle, grateful and docile, although constantly fearful lest You withdraw Your hand and they lose Your loaves. But You did not want to deprive man of freedom and

You rejected this suggestion, for, You thought, what sort of freedom would they have if their obedience was bought with bread?" [1]

Dostoevski accurately portrays the shattering power of eros. Eros dazzles a crowd with angels; it transforms rocks miraculously into bread. But Jesus was not interested in authenticating his power through demonstrations of this sort. That was not the way he intended to touch, to win over, the hearts and minds of people. Instead, he was, and still is, interested in making his authority evident in a way that preserves both his own freedom and the freedom of individual men and women down through the ages.

In *The Screwtape Letters* C. S. Lewis also reflects on Jesus' refusal to use his power to compel our allegiance. Screwtape complains to his nephew Wormwood that he simply cannot understand why God does not make more use of the power that is obviously his. He can't understand why God does not take away the will of those who choose to follow him. "You must have often wondered," he says, "why the Enemy [God] does not make more use of His power to be sensibly present to human souls in any degree He chooses and at any moment. But you now see that the Irresistible and the Indisputable are the two weapons which the very nature of His scheme forbids Him to use." [2] Screwtape can't figure it out. Jesus baffles him. Jesus has a better strategy than the irresistible and indisputable argument.

God never proves himself to anyone. If we constantly ask God to give us definitive proofs of his existence, we come away continually disappointed. God has no intention of taking away our wills. He does not paint us into a corner from which we can't walk away. It is ironic that throughout the history of the church we Christians have found ourselves often praying specifically for this very thing and then have wondered why God didn't come through with the answers we thought we wanted. Sometimes we've even wished upon ourselves experiences or signs which have the effect of overriding our wills, just because we so desperately have wanted them. But we misunderstand God's intent for us when we ask for the overriding of our minds and our doubts and our real thoughts. God's kingly reign doesn't win our allegiance in that way. He is not about to cancel us out even though we, at first, may resent this freedom in our relationship with him. "He who has ears to hear, let him hear" (Matt. 11:15). That is the posture Jesus assumes, and it is a posture which preserves our freedom and our personal integrity.

Jesus rejected Satan's temptations to capture the senses of the people he came to win to discipleship. Quite to the contrary, Jesus understated himself throughout his whole ministry. Even his resurrection from the dead is understated. Think about it. The resurrection of Jesus Christ, which was the most profound miracle ever to occur in the history of mankind, was a quiet event witnessed by only a few common people. There was really nothing spectacular about it—nothing to dazzle the senses of the world. And it happened in such a way, moreover, that makes it impossible to prove. One empty grave is like any other empty grave. Only a few people were even associated with that history-changing event. Jesus Christ, even in his own resurrection, even in his own victory over death itself, did not overpower his followers. How very sure he is of himself!

Don't misunderstand me. The love of God *is* wonderful and powerful. It has a profound beauty about it. But God's love goes far deeper than ecstasy. It is precisely this depth and excitement in agape love that produces what the New Testament writers call *chara*—joy. This is, perhaps, the closest synonym in the New Testament vocabulary for *erōs*. God's love does produce exhilaration in our lives. It can make us "high" in a very good and healthy sense. The agape experience can fill us with an indescribable exuberance. But it is not used to attract our attention in the first place.

Now, let's ask another specific question. Will experiencing the love of God narrow our lives? Will God's love draw us into some sort of sheltered island of security? Will it pull us into an exclusive family or some special inner group unrelated to all the rest of the human order? Will receiving the love of God have a shrinking effect on our lives? Will we be encouraged toward irrelevance? Again, there are times when we ask specifically for this kind of love—a love that will be exclusively ours, a love that will give to us a kind of support that comes from failsafe security, from in-group exclusiveness, from interior isolationism.

The desire for exclusiveness runs very deep in the human experience. It was altogether natural for the villagers of Nazareth to expect special favors because of their special relationship to Jesus. They were offended at Jesus, not because he spoke the words of Messianic fulfillment, but because he would not honor the ancient formula of philia love—special favors for those with special connections. Jesus did, in fact, love the people of his native place but not in the provincial sense they expected.

Perhaps essentially what we think we are going to receive from agape love is a kind of careful extension of our own immediate circle, a filling out of ourselves in a larger community of fellow believers. But the love of God as it is expressed in Jesus Christ is going to take us far beyond that. Jesus says, "But I say to you, Love your enemies and pray for those who persecute you" (Matt. 5:44). What unsettling words for the disciples to hear! For us to hear! How these words pose a profound challenge to philia love. It's so easy to love within the circle of companions who form our support group. Jesus, though, claims that his love encompasses a far broader territory than family members and the select friends with whom we have natural ties. It extends to people with whom we have no apparent ties whatsoever. God's love extends even to our enemies. The proportions of this love are so much greater than the mutual loves around which we so often organize our lives. Agape love stretches the limits of our world. Because of this stretching we are never expected to love apart from being loved in the first place by God himself. *"Beloved, let us love one another"* (1 John 4:7).

But if we really want to enter into this agape adventure, if we really are to be part of Jesus' family, we must love those whom he loves. Jesus Christ calls us to become involved in a love experience that brings our basic nature into tension. In some ways, it is like a deep, swift river. We would never have imagined it, much less have entered it willingly, had not we met Jesus. God's love may have implications that are somewhat foreign and strange and hard to handle at first. In fact, agape is the love we are likely never to become used to.

What happens when we welcome God's love into our lives? What happens when we decide to begin the adventure with agape? Well, as we have seen, at least two of our primary love expectations—the phileo expectation and the eros expectation—will be radically challenged and placed in a new perspective. And a completely new world view will emerge for us. That expanded world view will necessarily cause us to rearrange our lives so that many more people enter our circle of care and concern, even people with whom it seems at first that we have little natural affinity.

And, of course, along with his new kind of love goes a promise—through it all we will be experiencing an exciting, growing, person-to-Person relationship with the very One who created and redeemed us and who has loved us all along. In short, we become new people with a new life. This is the agape experience.

Love has its reasons . . . a thousand things declare it.[3]

Notes

Chapter 1

1. C. S. Lewis, *The Four Loves* (New York: Harcourt, Brace and Company, 1960), p. 17.
2. Ibid., pp. 17–18.
3. C. S. Lewis, *Mere Christianity* (New York: The Macmillan Company, 1953), p. 140.
4. C. S. Lewis, *The Horse and His Boy* (New York: The Macmillan Company, Collier Books, 1954), p. 157.

Chapter 2

1. Ethelbert Stauffer, *"Agapaō."* In *Theological Dictionary of the New Testament*, edited by Gerhard Kittel and Gerhard Friedrich (Grand Rapids: Wm. B. Eerdmans, 1964), 1:35.
2. Ibid.
3. Ibid.
4. From this point on eros and philia will be treated as English words, except where they are referred to specifically as Greek words.
5. Edward Steichen, *The Family of Man*, (New York: Maco Magazine Corp. for the Museum of Modern Art, 1955), p. 152.
6. Genesis 37:19 (KJV).

Chapter 3

1. Stauffer, *"Agapaō,"* p. 37.
2. Ibid, p. 39.
3. From this point on agape will be treated as an English word, except where the Greek word is specifically referred to.

Chapter 4

1. Robert Frost, "Mending Wall," *The Complete Poems of Robert Frost* (New York: Holt, Rinehart and Winston, 1947).

Love Has Its Reasons

2. Blaise Pascal, *Pensées*, trans. William F. Trotter (New York: Random House, Inc., 1941) p. 87, *Pensée* #245.

Chapter 5

1. C. S. Lewis, *Prince Caspian* (New York: The Macmillan Company, Collier Books, 1951), p. 36.
2. Dietrich Bonhoeffer, *Letters and Papers from Prison*, rev. ed. (New York: The Macmillan Company, 1967), p. 163.
3. Ibid., p. 14.

Chapter 6

1. Malcolm Muggeridge, *Something Beautiful for God* (New York: Harper & Row, 1971), p. 28.
2. Ibid, p. 22.
3. James W. Angell, *Yes Is a World* (Waco, Texas: Word Books, 1974), p. 77.
4. Muggeridge, *Something Beautiful for God*, p. 28.
5. See Luke 15:7.
6. Muggeridge, *Something Beautiful for God*, p. 28.
7. Ibid.

Chapter 7

1. C. S. Lewis, *The Screwtape Letters* (New York: The Macmillan Company, 1951), p. 37.

Chapter 8

1. Fyodor Dostoevski, *The Brothers Karamazov* (New York: Bantam Books, Inc., 1970), p. 304.
2. Lewis, *The Screwtape Letters*, p. 46.
3. "The heart has its own reasons which Reason does not know; a thousand things declare it." Blaise Pascal, *Pensées*, translated by H. F. Stewart in *Pascal's Pensées* (London: Routledge and Kegan Paul, 1950), p. 343. In Stewart's edition, this *pensée* is #626. In the translation by W. F. Trotter (Everyman and Modern Library), it is #277.